MW01233396

The Devotional Tales

50 Devotionals of the Christian's Love

By

Nick Shelton

authorHOUSE™

1663 LIBERTY DRIVE, SUITE 200
BLOOMINGTON, INDIANA 47403
(800) 839-8640
WWW.AUTHORHOUSE.COM

First published by AuthorHouse 11/16/04

ISBN: 1-4208-0797-8 (e)
ISBN: 1-4208-0795-1 (sc)
ISBN: 1-4208-0796-X (dj)

Library of Congress Control Number: 2004098225

Printed in the United States of America
Bloomington, Indiana

This book is printed on acid-free paper.

Table of contents

Preface from the Author

What is *The Devotional Tales*

I wrote my book, *The Devotional Tales*, to inspire one to develop a stronger Christian faith. In each chapter or devotion, I have written an inspiring/educational "tale" followed in depth discussing over some topic that I brought up in the story.

There is no specific audience to which these devotionals are addressed; although, I think it may appeal more to younger adults and upper teens. Regardless if you have been a devout Christian for 35 years or a nineteen-year-old teenager who has never been close to God, I believe reading this book will dramatically impact you. I believe the reason why this book may have a universal and powerful impact, is because the book's central focus is love. Love is something we all long for; love is the most powerful thing in the world; and love is what I writing about to you. The love that I write to you about is something that all want to have, but few have experienced – it is the Love of God.

What should I Get out of reading *The Devotional Tales*?

As a writer, I have tried to bring you an inspiring devotional that will change your life and how you live it each day. There are a lot of devotional books out there nowadays, so what sets this one apart? Well, from the many devotional books that I have read, I have found that many are boring or lack the inspiration needed to apply it

vii

to your life – it is though you read them, but they do not sink in and you are just reading words. However in *The Devotional Tales*, I have tried to make each lesson compelling enough to have a dramatic effect on your life. Although, it may not be a devotional that is a quick read for you, I believe if you take fifteen minutes to read a chapter in the morning or during your lunch break, that your time reading this book will be enough to change your life.

How should I read *The Devotional Tales*?

I recommend that you take the fifteen or so minutes each day to read *just one* chapter. I suggest that you read it in the morning or as early in the day as you can, so that you will be able to dwell on what learned throughout the day, as well as to put the things that you learned into practice while they are still fresh in your mind. The process for reading each chapter is simple. First, read the story or "tale" and take a moment to reflect on it. Then, read where I have gone into farther insight about specific topics from the tale. In my writings, I ask several questions to you. Some of the questions are self-evident or may seem rhetorical, but others I have intended for you to take some time to put some honest thought in answering. I suggest that you would write them down (you can find a notebook, legal pad, or come up with your own way with keeping with your own reflections/what you have learned) or at least take a little time to think about them in your head. Each day I have tried to leave you with having a sense that you have learned something about God and how He wants you to live your life. At the end of each lesson, I have listed around four or five scriptures that apply to the subject. You do not have to read the scriptures right after you read the rest of the devotion; as matter of fact, I suggest that you would read the scriptures at a latter time in the day (i.e. lunch or before you go to bed). This way, the scriptures remind you what you have learned from the day's lesson and it will act as a reminder for you to do what you have learned. I did not include a prayer at the end of each chapter, but I recommend that you would pray to God after you read the chapter, and especially pray in the area that the devotional touches you and pray that each devotional would bring you closer to God. I also do not encourage you to skip around in the chapters, but rather reading the devotionals in the order that they appear, even taking more than one day on a given chapter if you feel that you need to, if that devotional covers an area in which you struggle, or if the devotional was one that especially touched you.

Promise of Imperfection

I have tried my best to make this a non-denominational writing that comes straight from what I have learned from the Bible. I have continually prayed to God, asking that what I write would not be of my own understanding but would be according to His Word and Will. However, I am human; and like any other human, I am not perfect. So, everything in the book may not be perfect. If you come across an idea that you disagree with me about, I would love to hear from you (there are a multiple links that allow you to contact me about some issue in the book at The Devotional Tales' Website – **www.TheDevotionalTales.com**).

Grammatically, I know I have written many sentences that would have made my English teacher cringe, but I mainly concentrated on getting get my point across, rather than focusing on what sounds right or correct (in fact that sentence is grammatically incorrect in several ways). While I would rather keep my original text as it is now, if you do happen to come across an obvious grammatical mistake, I would love for you to send in any corrections to The Devotional Tales website.

The website
www.TheDevotionalTales.com

I encourage you to visit the website. The website allows me to interact with you the reader. I really want to hear from you – ask me for any advice; tell me if you do not understand a particular subject, tell me of ways the devotionals have impacted you or changed your life, or inform me in anyway that I can help you – I want to show that I care for you, and I will do the best that I can to help out a Christian brother/sister or do something to further the kingdom of the Lord.

The Tales

Each devotion begins with a tale. Each tale is approximately 400-500 words, and they serve as an introduction for the idea conveyed in each chapter. Some of the tales are real-life stories, while some are only real in the world in my head. I have used stories from all walks of life. The tales are what set this work apart from all the many other devotional books out there. I hope you enjoy them.

Bible Scriptures

All the scriptures listed at the end of each devotion came from the New International Version of the Bible. I picked the NIV as my weapon of choice (I will talk about the Bible being like a sword in some of the devotions), since it seems to be the most popular translation today. I decided to stick with just one translation because I do not like how some writers (especially in devotionals) use many different translations; they seem to make a verse fit into their lesson. I have tried to pick out scriptures that are closely related to the scripture. Once again if you know of a scripture that you think fits better than the ones I have listed; write to me using the link on the website.

I Encourage You to Use these Passages

I do not mind if you quote or use my devotionals, especially if you using it to inspire others. If you would like to use a tale in a sermon or speech to others, go ahead and do so. If you would like to read a chapter as a devotion to a crowd, go ahead. In matter of fact, how I got started in writing devotionals was by writing them to give as a morning devotion. However if you do read one out loud, I suggest that you shorten it a little, cutting out that which is not relevant to your audience or modifying the words so that it applies more specifically to your audience. (In the future, I plan on coming out with an edition that is especially for speeches and reading to groups of people – having bigger and easier to read font, having material taken out so that each devotional could be used as a five minute speech, being on a paper where one could easily modify the words to better fit their audience, and having footnotes and notes in the margin which give hints and ideas on how to make that specific passage a perfect speech.) You can do anything you want with my devotional except print it out and sell it. I would be grateful for the courtesy of you mentioning my name and *The Devotional Tales* any time you use it for any purpose.

Now that I have gotten all the boring stuff out of the way, I would like to wish you a great time reading this book. I have been praying for you and wish that your life would be impacted by God's message. May Christ's love fill you, as you grow to love Him more.

Tragedy Strikes

On April 19th, 1995 at 9:01 A.M. tragedy struck America when the Murrah Federal Building in Oklahoma City collapsed. Around a thousand people were in the building on the day of the bombing. One such person was David Miller, who was a seven-year-old boy who attended the daycare facility held in the building. Upon hearing the news John Miller, David's father, frantically left his office in an Oklahoma City suburb and rushed to the scene. John ran up towards the debris where he was quickly stopped by several government officials who stated, "Sir, you cannot go in there."

John forcefully exclaimed, "It's my boy, he's in there."

"I'm sorry, sir, firefighters are doing the best they can in there."

Another official added, "There's electrical fires, asbestos, and a chance of more rubble collapsing, so you would only be endangering your own life."

However, the officials saw the look in John's eyes and knew that there was no stopping this man. So, they lifted up the yellow tape and said, "Be careful." John searched tirelessly for his son. For hours he pulled back large chunks of concrete calling, "David, David – are you there?"

12 hours passed, 24 hours passed, and after 36 hours, the chief fireman went up to the father and said, "Sir, your courageous efforts have greatly inspired me and my men; I'm sorry you could not find

your boy, but at least you can go home knowing that you tried your best, and you did everything you could."

But John jerked back and replied, "I am going to keep searching until I see my son one more time whether he is alive or dead."

38 hours passed and finally one of John's "David" calls was answered by a barely audible "Daddy." John knew that this was the voice of his son. John pushed back large pieces of rubble that, in any other circumstance, would have taken at least three men just to budge. Then when John reached his son, he saw 12 other children trapped in a triangular wedge. John led the other children to safety and embraced his thought-to-be gone son. A local newspaper reporter heard John and David's story. The reporter went up to the seven-year-old David to ask him a few questions.

The reporter asked, "How was it down there?"

David replied, "A lot of my friends were scared and started crying and stuff, but I didn't cry though."

"Why was that David?"

"I knew my daddy would come for me – he promised that he would always be there for me."

In our lives God is searching (just like David's father) for you. Our Father promises us each day that He loves us and that He will always be there for us. In our lives we too should trust God and abide in his love. This love will be the central message in the chapters ahead, and I want nothing greater than for this love to become more alive in you.

In most of our lives up to this point, we wanted to do everything ourselves; it's been all about one person, that being ourselves. However, we must find that God loves us, and that He "will always be there for us." He will be there with us, from times when the rubble comes crashing down in our lives, to times when no one seems to care for us, from times when we are lost in life, to times when we are burdened with stress – He will always be there, always showing us His love.

Having this love will fully make our lives joyous and complete. Because it is amazing – our Father in Heaven loves us even more than this father love his son. For it is only when you feel or comprehend this love – that you fully understand what it is to be a Christian.

Ask yourself right now, have you felt this amazing love of God?

What does that love mean to you? (I ask you write this answer down now, so that you may look back later.)

Has this love changed your life?

We can have nothing greater than the love of the Lord in our lives, and we can do nothing greater in our lives than to express this love.

1 John 4:16,17 And so we know and rely on the love God has for us. God is love. Whoever lives in love lives in God, and God in him.

Psalm 33:5 The LORD loves righteousness and justice; the earth is full of his unfailing love.

2 Thessalonians 3:5 May the Lord direct your hearts into God's love and Christ's perseverance

Hebrews 13:5b, because God has said, "Never will I leave you; never will I forsake you."

1 John 4:8 Whoever does not love does not know God, because God is love.

Knowing Where Your Life is Going

On January 22, 2002, Michelle Hammond opened up an e-mail that read:

Dear Tom,

Great to hear that you are feeling great in the Lord now. It's so strange... you were feeling the same way that I was on Sunday. I had some problems myself and could not release myself during worship, and it was only after service that I felt God doing a work in me.

Tom, this is my sixth month here in this country. God has been so good to us in so many ways. He's been so good. But there is a major issue that I am trying to deal with.

Back in India, although I had a job in the secular field, I was so involved in ministry. If the church doors were open I would be there. I was working with the young people in our church there and now here all I find myself doing is going to church on Sunday. I am so ashamed to admit that I am not involved in any avenue of ministry. Maybe this is what God wants me to go through right now - Waiting for His will and purpose.

So please keep us in your prayers. I know I have a call of God on my life and this is not a good phase of life that I am going through.

Would appreciate your prayers.

May God bless and all that you touch be blessed today

In His Grace,

Sujo

8:15 a.m. Sept. 11, 2001 [1]

This may seem like an everyday e-mail from one Christian friend to another, but what Michelle went on to read was that this was written on the 83rd floor of the North Tower on the day of the 9/11 terrorists' attacks. Minutes later, Sujo was faced with an airplane that crashed just a couple of floors above him. Sujo and the rest of his coworkers raced for safety. Although at times Sujo was unable to move or see, somehow he was able to find a path to freedom. He would step out of the building just seconds before its collapse. Although he was covered in debris and mildly injured, Sujo was able to avoid disaster.

Sujo John came from a middle-class family, being an only child after his younger sister died of cancer at a young age. The boy was raised in Calcutta, India where the population is 20 million people, just in that one city. A missionary who had set up a Church in his hometown, led Sujo to Christ at age 15. Although the church at Calcutta was strong, Hindus still outnumber the Christians fifty to one. Sujo took his studies and his commitment with the church very seriously. He spent hours working with the poor in the community, including several times working for Mother Teresa. Though he was always working and serving, his education was always at the top of his list (he would get an MBA in Business Marketing and learn to speak 4 different languages). He moved to America just six months before his world would be turned upside down.

As one could hear in his e-mail, Sujo felt useless in being a Christian, and he prayed to God that he could in some way have an impact in those of this country. It's strange how God works sometimes – because in span of just 3 years, Sujo would go across the country sharing his story and leading many people to God. Just think if that one missionary had not converted Sujo to Christianity and how different things would be now. The hundreds of lives that have been changed after hearing Sujo's story would never have been. Or what if Sujo had given up hope and never prayed to God, asking to make him a person who would make a difference in the world – It is awesome how God works in our lives.

Since the days of 9/11, Sujo has appeared on television shows, has spoken to Church congregations and youth/school assemblies, has written another famous e-mail, and has written a book (*Do You Know Where are You Going?*) During a Christian television program, Sujo would get 417 people to walk up from the audience or call by phone, each saying that they wanted to live their life for Jesus. There is no telling how many others have been impacted by this man who prayed to God to somehow make a difference. Michelle Hammond opened up this forwarded email thinking she would delete it right away, but it ended up that her life would be forever changed. For that night, she would commit her life to Christ.

Sujo makes it a point in all of his speeches to speak about Jesus, not as a religion; but as the Way, the Truth, and the Life, in which believers have hope and are able to do the unimaginable. He stresses that only God can give us this peace, which we humans long for. At the end of his services, he always does an altar call, and he tells his listeners not to be influenced by the person next to them, because in India, he once forced himself to go up when he was not ready to become a Christian yet, so he always asks everyone to come up as their heart leads.

He wrote an email the day after the 9/11 tragedies. In it, he wrote to close family and friends, praising God and telling them that he survived. Sujo realized that he was almost taken away from earth, and he did not want another day to pass by without trying to reach out to his friends and relatives about Jesus Christ. Although it was only addressed to 12 people, this email has been forwarded countless times to places all over the globe. Dozens of people (including Michelle) wrote Sujo back, saying that his words in the letter would spur an interest in God, that would eventually lead these people to accepting Jesus in their hearts.

The email reads:

Dear friends,

It is my utmost privilege writing to you that I am alive and well. God graciously delivered me and my wife Mary from harm yesterday. The tragic events have not fully sunk in yet, but I have been reminded of the profound realization of the frailty of life. I have been given the starkest possible reminder that I needed to know where I was going in the next life. So this moment I want to just ask you "Do you know where you are going?" Jesus Christ has given me the peace needed to truly live my life. He has taken my broken heart and made my life have purpose and fulfillment. So I ask you my friends and relatives "Are you at peace with yourself." If not, please this day commit yourself to Jesus or write me back with any questions. It is not until you face death and see death in a loved one, that you fully realize the need for this Peace in your life.

May Christ fill your lives with this peace and joy, which can only come from Him,

Sujo John

I ask you now to pray the same prayer Sujo prays at the end of his speeches. Even if you have prayed this type of prayer hundreds of times, I ask that you would pray these words like you truly mean it. For we do not know when our last days on earth may be, so I ask that today you would give just one heart-felt prayer to God.

Dear Jesus,

Thank you for speaking to my heart. Lord Jesus, I am a sinner. I am sorry for my sins and for all the times that I have grieved Your heart. You took my place on the cruel cross, You died for my sins, and by Your blood I can have forgiveness for my sins. I receive You as my Savior. Lord, I thank You for eternal life, which You have promised for them that call upon Your name. I thank you Jesus for Your unconditional love.

In Jesus' name,

Amen

John 3:16 For God so loved the world that he gave his one and only Son, that whoever believes in him shall not perish but have eternal life.

Romans 4:24b-25 for us who believe in him who raised Jesus our Lord from the dead. He was delivered over to death for our sins and was raised to life for our justification

Nick Shelton

Ephesians 1:5-8 In love he predestined us to be adopted as his sons through Jesus Christ, in accordance with his pleasure and will— to the praise of his glorious grace, which he has freely given us in the One he loves. In him we have redemption through his blood, the forgiveness of sins, in accordance with the riches of God's grace that he lavished on us with all wisdom and understanding.

Revelation 2:10b Be faithful, even to the point of death, and I will give you the crown of life

[1] Source: *Do you know where you are going?*. John, Sujo. Lantern Books. September 2002.

Existence of God

A while back, I had a conversation with an uncle about God. But the thing you need to know about my uncle is that he is the type of person who is as stubborn as anything and can debate to a brick wall on why he is right. And being a very intellectual man, most of the time he is quite convincing. However, he is also an atheist, and this is where he and I clash. Time and time again, I have tried to start a debate and bring up the existence of God to him. But Uncle Jeff has thought his views through, and telling him that I believe in God because of the things which I've seen Him do in my life, is not very convincing. He simply comes back with a response of "having no proof," and God is merely a waste of time that humans made up to make the world "good". I would bring up how God answers my prayers and how I can "feel" God working in my life, but he would only come up with some deep thought that I could not come back to - let alone understand. So for several days, I went searching for solid proof of the existence of God, and I found the following things and told them to my uncle:

I started with the most obvious – our **own selves**. Just look at the human body it is so complex with all the systems of the body working perfectly together, with the miles of blood vessels, with the trillions of cells, with all the things that go on in one second – could we have possible evolved from one simple cell that supposedly just appeared out of nowhere?

Our Minds Look at our brain. In one second our brains process millions amounts of data, like right now it is forming the words you read into meaningful sentences, it is telling your muscles to hold a book and sit down, it is telling your heart to beat, and your stomach to digest. Science looks at this organ as any other organ: like the lungs breathe, the stomach digests, the liver secretes, and the brain thinks. But do you see your thoughts as a mere bodily function? And do you believe this complex, amazing 4 lb. organ just so happened to come into existence by chance?

The World Look at the world around you – we are on a planet that provides the right temperature, enough life-sustaining water, the right amount of oxygen, and so on – and all this happens in a perfect cycle so that it never runs out and supports life. If plants did not take in carbon dioxide and make oxygen there would be nothing for us to breathe, if the earth was as big as Jupiter, there would be no atmosphere for us to live in, if the earth were as close to the sun as Mercury, we could not survive the heat. So you mean to tell me how this planet is was perfectly made to support life, is a coincidence that came into existence by chance?

Our Conscience Look at how we as humans vary from culture to culture. We eat different foods, do different things to have fun, play different sports, talk different languages, etc; but what is considered right and wrong is basically the same everywhere. Murdering, stealing, lying are considered bad wherever you go. We don't kick kittens, push over old ladies crossing the street, or murder someone because we know this is bad, and everyone from everywhere knows this. Sociologists cannot explain this except that it must be from an inborn trait, considering maybe someone or something created us to know right from wrong.

Supernatural Who can explain all the things like angels that have no other explanations? We have all heard of stories like someone almost getting hit by a car but they felt a tug by a mysterious hand that caused them to go in the other direction. Or of a person telling someone to avoid a future accident, and it turns out that the person they talked to, was never really in existence. Or of Christians on their death beds crying "it is beautiful, it is beautiful," talking of what they see before they die. What other explanation, can one have about such things?

The Past How is it that people have believed in God since creation? Humans have always believed that some supernatural force created the world and rules over us. Alienated cultures, say like the Native American of this country, believed that there was a God in the sky that reigned over everything long before any European could set foot and told them about Christianity. Look at the billions of people who have given their lives to God – they have been some of the most intellectual, most influential, and most joyous people, no matter what there fate was here on earth.

Disproving the Bible No one can deny what took place in the Bible. In fact, many men have tried. But the more they tried to disprove it, the more they found that there was evidence of it. Someone tried to disprove Noah's arc, but he found the structure that supposedly is the arc - and get this - it was in a perfect ratio, having the dimensions of how a ship is supposed to be built, almost the exact ratio used by the U.S. Navy for their ships today. Others have found evidence of global flood that would date back to the time around Noah's time. Others have found meteorites around the site of Sodom & Gomorrah, land that appeared that showed the Red Sea separated, evidence of swarms of locusts in Egypt, evidence of the sun standing still correlating to a passage in Joshua, and countless other events, none of which can be disproved; and only supporting evidence was found.

Problems with Evolution If this world were a survival of the fittest like evolution claims, why do we see so many things like: men willing to lose their lives for their country, showing love even when it hurts, showing compassion because it helps another and not our selves, and dying for a cause. Come to think of it, these are the things we admire most – Isn't it strange that these were all the things Jesus did here on earth.

Archaeology As far as dating goes, it does not always appear to coincide with the Bible, but there is more archaeological evidence supporting people and events of the Bible, than there is going against it. For example archaeologists find much evidence supporting things like King David's great victories and his reign as king, but maybe once a year bones are found miles beneath the earth that are so obscure that one cannot even tell that they are bones. But these bones are portrayed as the sought after "missing link," and they make headlines. But it is the discoveries that we seldom hear about, which coincide with the Bible, that are found to be the truth.

Change in Heart How can someone change so much after accepting the gospel? It is not uncommon for a once drunk, drug addict, crook, or even murderer to completely change his life and become a loving, kind person. This not only shocks people when they see completely changed and better person, but it also goes against psychology and science which says that certain people are naturally evil and tend to have certain traits that will last for their lives.

Science Science has proved so many things, but when it comes to religion and existence of God; it is silent. It is actually impossible to determine what is good and evil scientifically. It is impossible to prove scientifically what we are required to do in life(or even in science for that matter). Science cannot explain life and what we are supposed to make out of it, but a Creator that gave us His Word through the Bible, can.

Power of the name of Jesus Why is it that when someone uses the name God or Jesus that attention or controversy always pops up? Movies have covered many controversial subjects and shown many graphic/shocking scenes, but the most talked about and controversial movies have been over Jesus. With all the many things going wrong in schools, the main complaint is whether prayer and the study of creationism vs. evolution should be allowed or not. It is said that 50% of Americans cannot properly define 3 or more words in our Pledge of Allegiance, but people have gone to much trouble to take the words "under God" out of it. How could just the name of Jesus and God alone have such an impact, if God were nothing more than something created in the mind?

Proof of everything else Do you realize that everything else in the world, people readily accept, but they don't accept God and Christianity in which there are countless examples in front of our eyes. For instance, one readily accepts that an automobile runs and moves people around. Though most people do not know what all is inside the hood of an automobile or how these parts work together to put a car in motion, they believe that the cars move – they do not need an explanation. However with God, people cannot accept Him, even though they can see Him move right in front of their face. We may not understand all about God or how He works, but anyone can see Him if they just open up their eyes and see the obvious.

Flaws in the Big Bang Things like: salinity of oceans not corresponding to number of years of earth's existence, having no evidence from key periods like the various ice ages, not knowing what caused the dinosaurs to be extinct supposedly millions of years ago; plus with many other facts that creationist scientists have pointed to in some of their arguments against the Big Bang and Evolution.

Feelings of other Christians All of these things I mentioned above all point to a Creator or God being for real, but the scientists and skeptics of this world want solid proof. There is no one that can give solid proof or show an experiment proving that God exists. But there is also no one who can give evidence or show an experiment proving that love exists. But ask anyone that has experienced either one, and they would tell you that there is nothing more real than either one of these things.

Misc. And there are so many other things that point to God, but they are way to numerous to include here or too long to explain. The evidence is out there, and for every Christian, everything in this world shows the existence of God.

These bits of evidence were enough to silence my uncle. A man that could argue anything, could not say a word to any of these facts. While he was not yet ready to convert to Christianity just yet, he said he would look more into the whole belief in the "God thing."

And he even said that he would be willing to go to Church with me one weekend.

So what about you; could you ever disbelieve God and believe we are all here because of chance? You can believe that everything in this world is all a mistake that never was meant to happen, but somehow did; or you can believe that we were created in this world perfectly with a plan and with meaning.

So many people today acknowledge God's existence - but they do not truly **believe** in God. To be a Christian in a few words would be: to *believe* in God, to *know* God, and to *love* Him. But so many people, even in our own community, never get past the first step.

Everyday we see the evidence of the existence of God, but everyday do we show the evidence that we **believe** in God?

Today, take the first step, and believe totally in God.

Job 19:25 I know that my Redeemer lives, and that in the end he will stand upon the earth

Psalm 50:7 Hear, O my people, and I will speak, O Israel, and I will testify against you:
I am God, your God.

Psalm 146:6 the Maker of heaven and earth, the sea, and everything in them— the LORD, who remains faithful forever.

Isaiah 40:28 Do you not know? Have you not heard? The LORD is the everlasting God, the Creator of the ends of the earth.

Isaiah 43:3 For I am the LORD, your God, the Holy One of Israel, your Savior

Isaiah 44:6 This is what the LORD says— Israel's King and Redeemer, the LORD Almighty:
I am the first and I am the last; apart from me there is no God.

John 8:54,55 Jesus replied, "If I glorify myself, my glory means nothing. My Father, whom you claim as your God, is the one who glorifies me. Though you do not know him, I know him. If I said I did not, I would be a liar like you, but I do know him and keep his word

John 14:1 Do not let your hearts be troubled. Trust in God; trust also in me.

John 16:30 Now we can see that you know all things and that you do not even need to have anyone ask you questions. This makes us believe that you came from God."

John 20:31 But these are written that you may believe that Jesus is the Christ, the Son of God, and that by believing you may have life in his name.

Romans 1:19, 20 Since what may be known about God is plain to them, because God has made it plain to them. For since the creation of the world God's invisible qualities—his eternal power and divine nature—have been clearly seen, being understood from what has been made, so that men are without excuse.

Ephesians 2:10 For we are God's workmanship, created in Christ Jesus to do good works, which God prepared in advance for us to do.

2 Timothy 1:12 That is why I am suffering as I am. Yet I am not ashamed, because I know whom I have believed, and am convinced that he is able to guard what I have entrusted to him for that day

Knowing God

Frank Swartz was a happy-go-lucky kid who seemed to love life and did not have a care in the world. Frank was an eighth-grader that was fairly popular in his middle school: he was a good athlete at all sports; he made good grades; and he was a good guy that got along with everyone in his class. Frank appeared to be living a perfect life, until one day when everything seemed to crash down on him at once.

Frank was outside shooting basketball in his yard, when he was interrupted by a police officer who walked up to him and asked, "Is this the Swartz residence?" Frank nodded his head and said, "Is there anything wrong, officer?" The policeman nodded his head and said, "It's your father," he then paused for a second and continued, "he was killed in a car wreck by a drunk driver, I'm sorry son." Frank did not know what to do - his world was turned upside down. He had just lost the person who he was closest to in life; the person who would play catch with him every night; the person who would say the prayers around the dinner table; the person who could always make him laugh when he was mad; and the father he loved.

Frank did not know why this had to happen; he wondered what he could have done; and he even resented God for what happened. For the next week in Frank's life, he hated God for all he went through, claiming God could have prevented his father's death. One night Frank got very emotional, screaming out, "Who are You

God?" "Why did You even create this world?" With his eyes full of tears, Frank cried, "Why did this have to happen?"

But just then something unexplainable happened. While saying these things, Frank with his eyes still full of tears looked up and saw the picture of Jesus on the cross, that had been in the hallway for years; except, this time when Frank looked up, he did not see arms nailed to a cross, but rather arms stretched out as if He were about to hug him. He did not see a face that was grimaced with pain, but rather eyes that were staring right at him, as if they were saying, "I love you." He did see a helpless man dying, but rather a man that was right there by his side. Frank then broke down and realized that even though he lost the world he once had, he now had a Friend that would be with him for the rest of his life. For the next 6 hours Frank read and read the Bible- it was as if he could not get enough – he wanted to know God more. Frank would later pray that night and accept Jesus into his heart.

Before that day almost everyone who knew him would have said that Frank was a Christian – he knew all the memory verses to memorize in Sunday School; he knew where to sit in Church every Sunday; he knew how to be a good kid; he knew what the holidays of Easter and Christmas were for; and he even knew what it took to be a Christian - but he did not **know** God. He was not a Christian because he did not really know God. He could quote dozens of Bible verses, but he did not really know Jesus as a friend; and he did not know how much God cared for him.

Frank would read the Bible every night and he grew to learn more and more about God. When Frank felt alone because he had no father, he was comforted with the thought that he has an Eternal Father in heaven who loves him more than he could ever imagine. Frank is still saddened by the loss of his father, but he now recognizes this as part of God's plan, and maybe it took an emotional event like this to make him the Christian that he is today.

In the previous devotional, I told you that being a Christian in ten words is: to *believe* in God, to *know* God, and to *love* Him. So most of us have no trouble in believing in God, but do you **know**

Him? You can say celebrate the birth and death of Jesus; you can take communion at Church; and you can try to do good - but do you really **know** God.

We claim to love God with all our whole heart: but do you **know** how do to this; do you **know** how to worship God; do you **know** how much He loves you; do you **know** His Word and what it tells you to do; do you **know** the Man who hung there on that cross; do you **know** what God has called you to do in your life; do you **know** enough to really love Him?

Jesus is our best Friend, Savior, and King; and we are supposed to love God more than anything else in this world – so don't you think we should get to know God more? He gave us the Bible to tell us all about Himself, and He gives us the privilege of praying to Him anytime we just want to talk. Think of your best friend or spouse and think of how much you know about them – you know what music they like, you know some of their deepest secrets, you probably know what they are doing this very second, and you sometimes know what they are going to say before they even say it. Do you know God like any other loved one in your life? While we can never fully understand God, we can know more about Him by having Him in our lives?

So you can believe in God, but do you know Him?

Ephesians 1:17 I keep asking that the God of our Lord Jesus Christ, the glorious Father, may give you the Spirit of wisdom and revelation, so that you may know him better.

Job 18:20 Men of the west are appalled at his fate; men of the east are seized with horror. Surely such is the dwelling of an evil man; such is the place of one who knows not God."

Galatians 4:8 Formerly, when you did not know God, you were slaves to those who by nature are not gods.

Colossians 1:10 And we pray this in order that you may live a life worthy of the Lord and may please him in every way: bearing fruit in every good work, growing in the knowledge of God,

How Great is Your Love

Lou Menn was the head of an illegal Christian group in Sholi, North Korea that numbered 23, including his wife and his two much-loved sons. The Communist North Koreans do not allow any sort of religion, and if any is found, the punishment is death. Lou Menn and the 22 other members literally dug out a tunnel in the ground for their secret meetings. While the candlelight was very dim, and Lou Menn was the only one to have a Bible - this small, cramped tunnel was a place of love. While these people had so little in wealth, they praised God for just being a part of His creation. Lou Menn would tell them that while they did not have much food, money, or freedom – they did have the love of the Lord – and each of these 23 Christians were as happy as a human could be. However, one day, as government officials were surveying land in the area, they came across the tunnel and Lou Menn's congregation. All 23 were immediately arrested and chained, as they were taken into a nearby city. There, they were cursed, spat upon, and beat with clubs. The head enforcement officer yelled to the group telling them to deny God; however, none of them would concede. The officer then joked, "Who is this God?" Lou Menn quickly responded, "He is the God we love; He is the source of Life; He is the one that has given us so much; He has created all that you see; He will wipe away ever tear; and …"

"Enough!" yelled the officer. "Well let's just see how much this God loves you and your family." The guards then proceeded to take Lou Menn's two sons Liu and Aya and another child from the group. They tied ropes around their small necks, as they walked them up the gallows. "Is this God worth your two sons?" questioned an officer. Lou Menn exclaimed, "They are just children, take my life instead." The officer said, "Then disavow God." But Lou Menn could not do it. So the head officer went to the children and said, "Anything left you have to say?" The little eight-year-old Liu looked his father in the eye and said, "I love you father, we will see you in heaven soon."

Then the children fell silently to their deaths.

The guard then turned to Lou Menn and said, "Last time, deny God or die," but Lou Menn and the others could not do it. So then the Koreans brought in a steamroller and had the Christians lie on the road chained in a line. The officer gave them a final chance and said that if one of the twenty-one Christians in the line would deny God, then all would be free. But as the steamroller inched forward no one tried to change their mind – no one even moved – all that was heard were the words of their lips singing the song that Lou Menn wrote, which says:

How Great is your love,
How Great is your love,

Your focus is the focus of our life
Bringing hope with things from above
To comfort all the tears and all the strife
With the greatest gift called love

This gift we give back to Thee
Giving ourselves as a part
Of a testament for everyone to see
This love in our heart

How Great is Your Love, Lord
Love that has forever changed me

In the last two devotionals, I said that being a Christian in 10 words is: to *believe* in God, to *know* God, and to *love* him. I explained how easy it is to believe in God and have suggested ways in which to know God, but how do we love God?

First look at what love is – think right now your picture of love.

The dictionary's meaning of love is:

A deep, tender, ineffable feeling of affection and solicitude toward a person, such as that arising from kinship, recognition of attractive qualities, or a sense of underlying oneness.

But when I think about love –

I think love is about wanting to be around someone no matter what the situation, love is when you would do anything for that person, love is what we think about when we daydream, love is that feeling deep down inside us that grips our heart that rules over our body, and love is having complete happiness and pure joy.

My idea of love is when Lou Menn showed that he would rather be with God, rather than live a life without torture; love is when Lou Menn would do anything just to stay right with God; love is when 23 N. Koreans huddled in a tight, dark tunnel just to hear the Word of God; love is when you are hungry and poor yet you have complete happiness and pure joy from the fact God is in your life; love is having a steamroller inch toward you, only to have your thoughts on the one thing that grips your heart.

The Bible emphasizes the importance of love, saying that love is the most important virtue. In fact, three of the most powerful words in the Bible is "God is Love"

How ironic that the three most powerful words in our language is "I love you."

I think being created in God's image we were created with the capacity to have this love in us. When we are able to obtain God's love in us, then we as Christians on a path to reach our ultimate goal.

Since the creation of man, the world has wondered what is the purpose of man.

In my opinion, the greatest thing which man can do is to love.

So this brings me to ask you the question - do you love God?
– Do you want to be around God no matter what the situation – say like having to spend more time with God, or giving up something you do on the weekend, or just wanting to be around God rather than things of this world?
– Do you want to do things for God – say like worshipping him every chance you get, praying to him more than once a day, reading his Word in your free time, and explaining the gospel to unbelievers?
– Do you think about God and what heaven will be like in your free time, instead of thinking about having lots of money, having the perfect spouse, or how you would rather be at a beach at this moment in time?
– Do you have that feeling that grips your heart that compels you to express love back to God? As we go throughout our busy day, do you have to force God in your life, or does your life force you to God?
– Do you feel complete happiness and pure joy when you are around God. Say like when you pray to God - do you feel in awe that you are talking to the creator of the universe. When you go to church are you joyful because you get to worship God. Would you picture yourself completely happy right now even if all your possessions and freedom would be taken away, but you still had God?

Clearly love is the most difficult step in becoming a Christian, but it is the most important.

I have already stated that love is the greatest thing that a human can do on earth, and this is why I think it has been the topic for thousands of songs, poems, and books over man's history. It is just what we want to do in life. I don't think it is a coincidence that it also just so happens to be: what God has forever shown upon us, and how we show Him that we want to be one of His followers.

So you can come up with your own definition of love and love can be however you want to describe it -
But that which you feel towards God — is it love?

John 4:7-11 Dear friends, let us love one another, for love comes from God. Everyone who loves has been born of God and knows God. Whoever does not love does not know God, because God is love. This is how God showed his love among us: He sent his one and only Son into the world that we might live through him. This is love: not that we loved God, but that he loved us and sent his Son as an atoning sacrifice for our sins.

Proverbs 10:12 Hatred stirs up dissension, but love covers over all wrongs.
Matthew 22:37-40 Jesus replied: `Love the Lord your God with all your heart and with all your soul and with all your mind.' This is the first and greatest commandment. And the second is like it: `Love your neighbor as yourself.'
1 Corinthians 13: 4-7 Love is patient, love is kind. It does not envy, it does not boast, it is not proud. It is not rude, it is not self-seeking, it is not easily angered, it keeps no record of wrongs. Love does not delight in evil but rejoices with the truth. It always protects, always trusts, always hopes, always perseveres.
Galatians 5:13 You, my brothers, were called to be free. But do not use your freedom to indulge the sinful nature rather, serve one another in love.
Colossians 3:14 And over all these virtues put on love, which binds them all together in perfect unity.
1 John 4:16,17 And so we know and rely on the love God has for us. God is love. Whoever lives in love lives in God, and God in him. In this

way, love is made complete among us so that we will have confidence on the day of judgment, because in this.

Sarus

I had a dream one night of a sports star who was the greatest athlete ever known. The dream took place during the year 2015. This man came from a small town, but he was eventually known worldwide. His name was Sarus, no first name or initial; he was simply known as Sarus. Sarus first made it big playing the nation's pastime, baseball. As a pitcher with an overpowering fastball, he was able to pitch dozens of no hitters, and every time he went up to the plate to bat, he was sure to hit a home run. The media wrote in frenzies about him, telling of all his record-breaking triumphs; fans came from all over to see him; and the name Sarus was as well-known in every American household as the name Coca-Cola is today. With his lightning-fast speed and great throwing arm, fans convinced this man to play quarterback for a NFL team. Success poured over from the baseball diamond to the football field when Sarus won the Super Bowl in his first year. Everybody came to see this man they called Sarus, everyone would ask, "Did you see what Sarus did last night?" and "What time is Sarus playing tonight?" People, who had never liked sports before, were now interested just because of Sarus, and every kid ages 4-14 wanted to play pitcher or quarterback to be just like Sarus. But after a short 3-year career, jealous athletes and crazed fans formed an angry mob and killed Sarus. However, after his death, his fame only grew, especially after his autopsy showed he never used any steroids or foreign substances.

Even then the jealous athletes agreed that this was the most talented man that ever walked the earth. He grew into a legend. Over the years his stories were constantly being retold, and his career was actually portrayed in a movie that would break all sorts of box office records. His diary he kept was published and sold well over 1 billion copies.

So could an athlete ever be as great as Sarus? Of course not.

But Jesus did.

In His 3 year ministry, throngs of crowds followed Him.

I am sure the talk of the towns was, "Have you heard of this man they call Jesus?" and "Did you hear what Jesus did yesterday?"

It was not until after His Death that most of the people realized that He was the man that He claimed to be.

The Bible, the book written about Him, has become the best-selling book of all-time.

Jesus has changed the lives of millions and millions of people throughout time, a number that is difficult for us to comprehend.

So what has caused this devotion to Him? It is not because people are afraid they may go to hell, it is not because these people's parent followed Him, it not because men in history glorified Him in their writings, and it is not because people turn to the supernatural to explain life – it is because of His love. It is only love that could have stood against time, nations, and all the world's evil. He loved everyone more than anything else in the world, and because of this love, He will always reign in people's hearts.

By accepting Jesus in our hearts, we as humans are doing the greatest thing that we can do – TO LOVE.

This man who could walk on water, heal the blind, and raise the dead - could have decided to save the world in many different ways, but he choose to do it out of love.

Therefore our purpose in life should be to accept Jesus' love and let our lives be filled with love.

Ask yourself right now, "What do I think about Jesus." Is He in your heart? Is He the Man written about in the Bible? Is He the Man that has changed millions of lives? Is He your best friend? Is He the One who you asked to take away your sin? Is He the person that you are striving to become? Is He your Savior?

The word *Jesus* is a powerful word throughout the world. Dozens die everyday because they confess Jesus as the Lord of their life. Millions of others spend their entire lives learning about this man. Millions confess that their ultimate goal in life is to become more like this man. To the millions that have never seen Him, He is easily recognized. Millions from all nations declare Him the King of their life. As John baptized Jesus in the Jordan River, millions are baptized every year. Although He never wrote a line, His book is the best seller of all-time. Although He only used words to teach, his lessons have impacted far more than any other teacher, professor, scientist, or philosopher. Although he never received a formal education, He has served to educate millions on life. Although his miracles were only seen by a selected few, millions now believe. In just three years, this man left the world with knowledge that will never be forgotten. In just three days, this man suffered, so that all the world's sins could be forgiven. Since the days that Jesus walked here on this earth, the world has yet to be the same.

Who is Jesus in your life?

Isaiah 9:6,7 For to us a child is born, to us a son is given, and the government will be on his shoulders. And he will be called Wonderful Counselor, Mighty God, Everlasting Father, Prince of Peace. Of the increase of his government and peace there will be no end. He will reign on David's throne and over his kingdom, establishing and upholding it with justice and righteousness from that time on and forever. The zeal of the LORD Almighty will accomplish this.

Matthew 14:33 Then those who were in the boat worshiped him, saying, "Truly you are the Son of God."

Mark 15:39 And when the centurion, who stood there in front of Jesus, heard his cry and saw how he died, he said, "Surely this man was the Son of God!"

Ezekiel 34:31 You my sheep, the sheep of my pasture, are people, and I am your God, declares the Sovereign LORD.' "

Matthew 16:16 Simon Peter answered, "You are the Christ, the Son of the living God."

Mark 14:61,62 Again the high priest asked him, "Are you the Christ, the Son of the Blessed One?"

"I am," said Jesus. "And you will see the Son of Man sitting at the right hand of the Mighty One and coming on the clouds of heaven."

Acts 10:36 You know the message God sent to the people of Israel, telling the good news of peace through Jesus Christ, who is Lord of all.

A Friend's Saving Power

Daniel Mills and Gary Staduamire were called to fight for their country in the Vietnam Conflict. The two men could not be more different. Daniel was a tall, skinny 19 year-old white male, who had just graduated high school and enrolled in the army. Gary was a strongly-built 32 year-old African-American prison guard who had been drafted into the army. Despite the differences, the two men became best friends while in Vietnam. The nights over there were cold from the monsoon-like rains, and since they had no shelter, the two men would sleep propped up on each other, keeping their bodies warm and heads off the muddy ground. Having a fear for the next day and shivering from the cold, the two guys did not sleep much. So they spent much of the night talking sharing life stories, opinions, memories, and things that they would never tell anyone else. Even on the battlefield the two would stay right beside each other. They would find a barricade to stand behind, and Daniel, the left-hander, would take the left side and shoot all the enemies on the left, and Gary, the right-hander, would take the right. You could be sure to hear a little bit of bragging in their night's conversations, if one took down more enemies than the other. Before every battle, Gary would turn to his friend and say in his deep voice, "I'll always be there for you, brother." And Daniel would shake his hand and say, "Me too, I'll always be there for you." One day as the two were marching through a rice field, a band of Vietnamese soldiers ambushed the

American soldiers. Somewhere in the confusion, young Daniel caught 2 bullets in his right leg. He was bleeding profusely and was unable to walk. Gary turned around and exclaimed to Daniel, "Get up man, we got to get out of here!"

"I can't Gary," showing him his leg, "I can't get up"

"Oh man, you need some help; I'll take you to the medic."

"No, you got to get out of here, leave me behind."

But Gary could not leave his best friend behind, so he attempted to carry his dying friend to safety. Gary hoisted Daniel up onto his broad shoulders, and ran about 25 yards before 3 bullets ripped through Gary's back, sending the big man to his knees, then to the ground. Daniel looking his friend in the eyes said, "I can never thank you enough"

Gary then took one last breath and said, "I promised you I'd always be there for you. I love you, man."

Daniel with tears in his eyes whispered to his friend, "I love you too, brother."

Daniel then crawled on his stomach all the way back to camp.

Daniel was eventually sent home with one less leg that he had when he went there, but even more costly, he had one less friend. Now at 55 years of age, Daniel tells his story, saying that Gray Staduamire was the perfect example of friendship. He says, "If we all had a friend like Gary that there would be: less arguing, more peace; less worrying, more enjoying; less crying, more comforting; less pain, more laughing; and overall more happiness in each of our lives."

Most will say that they do not have a friend like Gary that will risk their life delivering them from death in the midst of war. But actually, you do have that friend; a friend called Jesus. A friend who is willing to die for you, so that you may live; a friend who will always be there for you; a friend who you can always talk to, sharing even your deepest secrets; a friend who will pick you up when you are down on the battlefield; and a friend who truly loves you.

Look at anybody who truly has Jesus as their best friend; does their life show the characteristics that Daniel Mills says comes from having a **perfect** friend showing: less arguing, more peace; less worrying, more enjoying; less complaining, more comforting, less crying, more laughing, less pain, and more happiness compared to the rest of the world?

The definition of the word friend is: one attached to another by affection or esteem.

Do you see yourself as **attached** to Jesus? Is He your friend?

If you never really viewed Jesus as your best friend, ask Him today and see how much He can change your life. The next time you are depressed, hurt, anxious, or afraid - go to Jesus. He will help you go through anything in this world, and He will be right there with you, loving you until the end.

Psalm 25:14 The LORD confides in those who fear him; he makes his covenant known to them.

Psalm 144:2 He is my loving God and my fortress, my stronghold and my deliverer, my shield, in whom I take refuge, who subdues peoples under me

Job 29:4 Oh, for the days when I was in my prime, when God's intimate friendship blessed my house

Micah 6:8 He has showed you, O man, what is good. And what does the LORD require of you? To act justly and to love mercy and to walk humbly with your God.

The Meaning of Life

Elijah Donaldson was born to a struggling couple who had been married for 15 years. The Donaldsons rejoiced greatly for their blessing from God, and it did not take them long to find that God also truly blessed this child. The Donaldsons found that their son had an exceptional learning ability. Even at a young age, the sharp-minded boy usually out-smarted his parents. By age 10, Eli had won all the local spelling/geography bees, plus showed his talents by competing in the national events. By age 14, he graduated high school, and then went on to study at Hope Community College. There he went on to learn to speak three new languages: Spanish, German, and Latin. Plus, he would go on to gain Ph.D. degrees in mathematics, psychology, and philosophy in top-notch schools like the University of Virginia and Yale. His 182 I.Q. score certifies him as a true genius of the time, and he is known by some as the "smartest man in the world." After his schooling, he has used his mind and extensive knowledge of various subjects to write 29 books. At age 42, he became president of Browne University. There he found his future wife, and for the first time, he began to slow his life down from the intense studying, writing, and reading in order to start a family. At the university, Eli would even teach some of the classes in which he had a Ph.D. degree, some of which even used the textbooks that Eli had written years before. After years of teaching and being president at the university, Eli was confronted at the graduation ceremony by one of his favorite students, Calvin Kingston.

Calvin asked, "Dr. Donaldson you are one of the smartest men to ever live on this planet. As I have had the joy of learning from you the past 4 years, I feel I have learned so much, but since I am about to embark out into the world, I wanted to know about life."

"Life?" asked Eli.

"Yes sir, Dr. Donaldson, like 'What is the meaning of life?' What are we as humans supposed to do, have, accomplish; what is it all about?"

"Yes, life," Eli said out loud looking to be in thought, "You know Calvin, that's a deep question, could you give me your e-mail address, I'll get back to you on this one."

Three months later on August 30, 1999, Calvin received an email from Dr. Donaldson that read:

"Calvin,

I bet you thought that I had forgotten about your question, but actually I have been thinking about it all this time. The following are things in which I have learned, thought about, and came up with:

- I've found the more I learn in life, the more I find that I do not know about it.
- To answer the question, "Does a falling tree make a sound if no one is there to hear it" – Well it will have a great thunderous noise if it is an oak tree, but if it is a birch tree it may make a small crack. People can be either oak trees or birch trees. Everyone falls; everyone fails. But how you fail makes the man. A man can be a high and mighty oak tree and think nothing can take him down, and when he does fall, he falls with a great thunder. Or, a man can be a birch tree in that when faced with the strongest winds, he just sways with the wind and maybe cracks a few branches, but after the wind is gone he is standing as tall as before. A key to life is being a birch tree.
- I've learned that IQ, personality, and self-esteem test may tell in detail all about people, but I've learned that you can learn

more from a person by the way they handle three things: a rainy day, lost luggage, and Christmas tree lights.

- I've learned that life is like a box of chocolates – Everyone will have pieces that they like and some they do not. It's just like a person or a book; you can not tell what you are getting by looking on the outside, so you must try to see if you like it. And no matter what you get, be optimistic and do not let the bad ones upset your image of the whole box (life).

- Friendship works good in mathematics, it doubles our joy and divides our grief.

- I've learned that if you pursue happiness, it will elude you. But, if you focus on your family, your friends, the needs of others, and doing the best you can – happiness will find you.

- I've found that a picture is worth a thousand words, a smile is worth more than a thousand words, an act of kindness is worth more than a thousand smiles, and love is greater than a thousand acts of kindness.

- A perfect world is found in our dreams; men's fondest dreams become their desires, yet man's desires are self-centered acts that lead to evil. I do not know where everyone gets off the original intention, but I've learned if you keep your desires on what is good, your path of life will be straight.

- I've found my life is like a jigsaw puzzle, and every time I receive an honor, reward, merit, prove a theory, solve an unsolved math problem, write a book, or gain some other accomplishment - I add another jigsaw piece to the puzzle. However the more I pieces I add, the more space that is left to fill as if I were only adding the end pieces and not the heart of the puzzle. But why would I want an incomplete jigsaw puzzle when I could have a perfect portrait of someone else?"

Below was a picture of Jesus hanging on the cross.

Calvin if you do not follow any of my other maxims, be sure you follow this last one, because no matter what, God can deliver you

The Devotional Tales

out of any situation in life, and He will provide all that is needed in your life.

And if I'm not smart enough for you to trust me, listen to this quote of Einstein: "When you examine the lives of the most influential people who have ever walked around us, you discover one thread that winds through them all. They have been aligned first with their spiritual nature then with their physical self."

So Calvin, your answer to "what is the meaning of life" – It is a chance to know the God who is, was, and forever will be.

Your friend and teacher,
Dr. Donaldson

Life is a collection of things that you can do, visit, see, get, and accomplish, but have you found it's meaning?

2 Samuel 7:22 How great you are, O Sovereign LORD! There is no one like you, and there is no God but you, as we have heard with our own ears.

Psalm 37:5,6 Commit your way to the LORD; trust in him and he will do this: He will make your righteousness shine like the dawn, the justice of your cause like the noonday sun.

Habakkuk 3:18,19 yet I will rejoice in the LORD, I will be joyful in God my Savior. The Sovereign LORD is my strength; he makes my feet like the feet of a deer, he enables me to go on the heights

I Corinthians 3:22,23 and you are of Christ, and Christ is of God.

The Heart of a True Champion

Dimitrius Alaizaar went to the 1975 International Running Championships hoping to bring home a gold medal to his home country of Greece. Greece is known as the origin of the first international sports competition (the Olympics), but the country had yet to win a gold medal in any kind of international event since 1952. Dimitrius, having a pride in his country and the competitive nature of a true athlete, devoted four years of his life to train for the most grueling event of the games, the marathon (Ironically, Greece is also well-known for being the originator of the marathon, but they had not won a title in this event since the first Olympic games).

Dimitrius knew what he had to do to train his body - for five years, he ate nothing but the healthiest foods along with running four to five hours, swimming, lifting weights, stretching, and jumping rope. Dimitrius literally spent all day training his body to be in top shape.

Finally on July 17 on a hot summer day in Barcelona, Spain, Dimitrius got his chance to obtain his goal. In order to win, Dimitrius would have to outrun the much-touted runners from the African countries, such as Kenya and Ethiopia, that dominated the sport.

The gun was fired, and the runners were off. Dimitrius went out and gained an early lead at the third mile. Dimitrius was running great, but could he keep up that pace for another 23.2 miles.

Dimitrius would maintain his lead until the last mile of the race, when he realized that he had nothing left in him to finish the race. He looked back and saw a pack of Kenyan runners briskly advancing towards him – none of them showing any signs of fatigue. Dimitrius' heart felt like it could not beat any longer, his body ached at every point so that he could not feel a difference from one pain from another, his mouth was dry, his vision blurred, and he could not concentrate on anything but the pain. Yet in the back of his mind he knew what he would have to do in order to win. In the end, Dimitrius gave one last surge for that last mile and crossed the finish line just ahead of his competitors, as a crowd of spectators erupted with cheers as they watched one of the closest finishes in marathon history. However, Dimitrius Alaizaar never heard those cheers, nor see his gold medal, nor get to celebrate with his countrymen. For Dimitrius died instantly, collapsing after crossing the finish line. The result was due to heart complications. Later that heart would get recognized worldwide as: "A Heart of a True Champion."

Dimitrius managed to do what he wanted – he brought the mark of a champion back to **his** homeland.

Jesus Christ in the same way went through another grueling experience on the cross for the sake of **His** people.

He died a painful death, and had nothing to show for it except His love for us.

Dimitrius knew what he had to do to win; he had a committed attitude and a love that would endure any pain. Dimitrius' story is one we love to see and hear. When we watch a sporting event such as the Olympics or the National Championship of a given sport, we wait to see such performances. We want to see the athletes who want more than anything, just to be there; athletes who overcome the odds; athletes who love to play the game, and athletes who give it their all. These athletes dedicate countless hours of their life preparing for the glory of that one moment and for a chance to be called a champion.

In Jesus' life on earth, he spent his time preparing for that one moment – that one moment that would change history. He gave it his all; suffered the pain; and defeated the sins that keep us from Him.

In our lives, we should want to become like Jesus in this way. We may not have that "one moment," but we should be willing to endure any pain and give all we have to Christ Jesus our Lord.

Just like we await to see these athletes compete with all their heart, God wants nothing more than from us than to show a likewise manner in living a life for Him.

He wants to see us wanting more than anything just to be with Him; He wants to see us overcoming the odds; He wants to see us loving our life in Him, and He wants to see us giving it our all.

If you commit your life to such a goal, you will live your life like a "true champion."

1 Corinthians 9:24-27 Do you not know that in a race all the runners run, but only one gets the prize? Run in such a way as to get the prize. Everyone who competes in the games goes into strict training. They do it to get a crown that will not last; but we do it to get a crown that will last forever. Therefore I do not run like a man running aimlessly; I do not fight like a man beating the air. No, I beat my body and make it my slave so that after I have preached to others, I myself will not be disqualified for the prize.

Philippians 3:12,14 Not that I have already obtained all this, or have already been made perfect, but I press on to take hold of that for which Christ Jesus took hold of me.

I press on toward the goal to win the prize for which God has called me heavenward in Christ Jesus.

2 Timothy 2:3 Endure hardship with us like a good soldier of Christ Jesus

Hebrews 12:1-3 Therefore, since we are surrounded by such a great cloud of witnesses, let us throw off everything that hinders and the sin that so easily entangles, and let us run with perseverance the race marked out for us. Let us fix our eyes on Jesus, the author and perfecter of our faith, who for the joy set before him endured the cross, scorning its shame, and sat down at the right hand of the throne of God. Consider him who endured such opposition from sinful men, so that you will not grow weary and lose heart.

The Sherman Project

On September 30, 1960, Matthew Sherman listened to a moving sermon in church that stressed even the smallest works done out of love would lead to something so much greater. Matthew decided to follow his pastor's advice by initiating a project which he would follow one good deed and tract its process to see if it would have a wave effect. He called it the Sherman Plan. Basically the Sherman Plan was for Matthew to do 3 acts of kindness to others each week, and then Matthew would ask that person to likewise do 3 acts of kindness of equal or greater measure; and if the person would, tell him the deed so that he could record them (a similar principle was found in the 1996 movie *Pay It Forward)*. On the first day, that Monday, Matthew woke up to a rainy, dreary day. He got ready and went to a local restaurant for breakfast. In the restaurant, Matthew asked the man on the stool beside him, if it would be ok if he paid for this man's breakfast, as long as the man would agree to do three equal or greater act of kindness. The man had to think about it for sometime, thinking it may be some kind of trick, but he eventually agreed.

During Matthew's lunch hour as he walked down the sidewalk, he watched a man get drenched from a car splashing up water and mud from a puddle on the street. The young man's clothes were all messed up. Matthew quickly went up to the young man and said, "I'm sorry about that, your clothes are probably ruined, but I'll tell you what – you look about my size. I've got plenty of old suits at my house, and I only live a few minutes away. I'd be glad to give you a couple of mine just out of kindness." The young man named James thought it was kind of weird how Matthew was so friendly, but he was a young man that was looking for a job, so he took Matthew's invitation. Matthew had several suits at home that were now too small for him, that fit James perfectly. James asked how he could thank him, but Matthew responded that there was no need to thank him, just to do 3 equal or greater acts of kindness to someone else.

After completing his day at work, Matthew returned home to see that his next-door neighbor was having a fence put up. He saw that one of the young workers putting up the fence had gotten a nail accidentally hammered into his thumb. Matthew quickly took the young man into his house to take out the nail, clean up the wound, and bandage his thumb. The 16-year-old boy, named Grey, thanked Matthew, but instead of saying "You're Welcome," Matthew told Grey to pass the good deed onto 3 other individuals.

The next day, Matthew came home to Grey building a doghouse for Matthew and his family. Matthew was very pleased at the young boy's talent and discipline for staying with the Sherman Plan. Matthew told Grey, "Wow, I'm, very impressed."

"Thank you, sir. I was only staying true to your advice."

"Well, Grey, I'd say that you have a heck of a talent building things; I think you should stick with your talent in the future." Grey took heed to William's advice: he built other small things for people, some for money and others just out of kindness – the latter he grew to love. Years down the road he became a professional architect building some of the elite homes of the community, yet after he made a successful living – Grey Allday starting building homes for those in need. He started his own organization based on volunteer labor and those wanting to do acts of kindness. With the help, he would build homes and homeless shelters across the nation. The organization, still strong today, has built over 250 homes and 100 shelters which has housed over 10,000 individuals.

And that man Matthew met at the restaurant. He would later return to that same restaurant for dinner that night, and he would pay for a lady's meal there. The man explained how he had promised to spread 3 gifts of kindness. The two would go on to have a long conversation that night. Three years later, the two would get married.

And James, who received the suit, went onto land a very successful business job, but in the process he decided to pass on his good deeds. James was a Christian and decided that there was no better act of kindness, than to reach out to fellow friends and people his age about the love of Christ. James led a 25-year-old friend from Kentucky, named Henry O'Donnell, to Christ. Henry's parents orphaned him at the age of two, and Henry had lived a rough life ever since. However, with his new love of Christ (inspired by James' commitment to pass forward the good deed), Henry O'Donnell traveled nationwide to orphanages across the country, to tell the children that he too was like them living in an orphanage without a true father or mother. He explained to them that there was a Father up in heaven that loved each and every one of them. He told them that God would never leave them and would always be there for them when they needed Him.

So in all, there was a man that brought Jesus into the hearts of hundreds of orphans, an organization that would build hundreds of houses for the needy, a marriage, plus other great things that would happen later down the chain of the Sherman Project that included: a high school graduate receiving a much needed scholarship to pay for college, a makeup between a husband and wife whose relationship was heading toward divorce, a clean up of a dilapidated, run-down park in the city, countless hours of volunteer work, a wedding ring being found and returned to the owner, and many other great acts of kindness.

Not bad considering all this came from taking care of a hurt thumb, paying a couple dollars for someone's breakfast, and giving away some old clothes that did not fit anymore.

It's amazing what can result when we do something out of love. Acts of kindness have a tremendous effect on the world. As Christians whose goal is to reach out to this world, our life should be full of kindness. We do not have to give something great; something like giving a smile, showing support, giving a compliment, and giving your time can be enough kindness to change people's lives. Many of us were not blessed with talents like being able to build a doghouse, the money to devote to charities, or time to do something "great" with our kindness, but what we do not realize is that any act out of kindness is great, no matter how small it is.

How have you showed kindness to others in the past?
In what ways could you show more kindness in the future?
I suggest that you would try to do your own Sherman Project every month, week, or day. You do not have to follow your three acts to see where they go, if you don't want, but make an attempt to show three acts of kinds and tell the person to spread the kindness on.

Doing good to others is contagious. Just like William Sherman's experiment, our kindness will be transmitted to others, who will catch this infection and spread it even more. Can you imagine what could happen if The Sherman Project was adopted widespread in our culture like some of the other popular fads of our day. Make it your priority to be the one who starts the fad of showing three acts of kindness.

Christ showed his love for the world by dying for our sins; we can show our love to the world by being kind to others.

Galatians 6:10 Therefore, as we have opportunity, let us do good to all people, especially to those who belong to the family of believers.

Zechariah 7:9 This is what the LORD Almighty says: `Administer true justice; show mercy and compassion to one another.
Romans 15:2 Each of us should please his neighbor for his good, to build him up.
Galatians 6:2 Carry each other's burdens, and in this way you will fulfill the law of Christ.
Hebrews 3:13 But encourage one another daily, as long as it is called Today, so that none of you may be hardened by sin's deceitfulness.

1 Peter 3:8 Finally, all of you, live in harmony with one another; be sympathetic, love as brothers, be compassionate and humble

Standing Up

A few years ago at a university in California, there was a professor who was a devout atheist. The professor, named Rodney Stone, taught a class of philosophy that's primary objective was to prove that God did not exist. Professor Stone would shout, "Whoever believes in God is a fool," in a deep, powerful voice that would echo in the auditorium that held 300 students. And no one would ever argue against this tall 6'7" professor. The students were intimidated by his stature and presence. Whenever he would walk into the room, immediately all 300 students became silent, and whenever he asked something to be done, a student would quickly stand up and say, "Yes sir, Dr. Stone," and do the task without hesitation. For 20 years, the professor taught the class, and no one ever had he courage to go against him. If any question was asked about the existence of God, the professor would just use profound logic and precise rhetoric to persuade to the class that there was no such thing as God. At the end of each semester, Professor Stone would say, "Alright it's time for the final exam." He paced around for a second and then asked, "If there is anyone here who still believes in God, stand up." The class sat in complete silence, and no one ever stood up. Professor Stone said, "Good, if anyone believes in God, they are a fool – then he wrote on the chalkboard: "God does not exist." – underlining the word *not* several times. "For if he existed," yelled the professor, "He could stop this piece of chalk from hitting the ground and breaking.

Such a simple task and he can't do it." Every year he would drop the chalk onto the floor, as it would shatter into a hundred pieces. For twenty years no one ever stood up – those 20 years Professor Stone taught over 12,000 students but none of them ever said a word in Professor's Stone so called final exam. While some believers managed to go through the course still believing in God, none of them ever had the courage to stand up and say they did, fearing that Professor Stone would ridicule them in front of everyone and would fail them in the class.

But a few years ago, in 1999, a freshman at this college named Tony Nichlaus happened to enroll in the class. Tony was a Christian, and he heard the stories of the professor, but he was forced to take the philosophy class because it was required in his major. So for three months, every morning before class, Tony would pray to God asking for strength so nothing the professor said could shatter his faith; and that his faith could cause at least one other person in the class to believe in God, even if it did cause him to fail the class. Finally, the day came and Professor Stone said, "It's time for the final exam," and once again he asked, "If there is anyone here that still believes in God, stand up." Tony which was exactly in the middle of the auditorium, stood up as 299 pairs of eyes turned and looked at him. Professor Stone shouted, "You Fool!" The professor's head turned red with anger, and he yelled, "If God existed, he would keep this piece of chalk from breaking." But as he proceeded to drop the chalk, it slipped out of his fingers, off his shirt cuff, onto the pleat of his pants, down his leg, and off his shoe. As it hit the ground it rolled away unbroken. The professor's eyes became wide, almost bulging out of his head, as he saw the piece of chalk intact. Then he looked up at Tony still standing, and the speechless professor ran out of the lecture hall.

Tony then got up and began to share his faith in Jesus to the whole room for the next half hour. While the students were free to go, all 299 stayed in the auditorium. At the end, Tony invited those who wanted to make a commitment to Christ to pray with him that day. Dozens and dozens of students (someone counted 98 people) got up to pray with Tony, committing right there that they not only believed in God, but also wanted Him to be in their life each day.

Isn't weird how God works sometimes? Tony prayed everyday for the courage to literally stand up for God. Tony not only stood up, but he had an impact on everyone in that room. Not bad considering he only prayed for his faith to have on impact on just one. Tony recognized that this was going to be a difficult ordeal to overcome in his life, but it would also be a chance to witness to others. That is why he prayed everyday for God to use him in the situation, and the situation be used to lead others to God. Tony did not pray that he would not fail the class or that he would not be made fun of by the professor/students; he simply wanted God to be known as the truth. We likewise should pray like this – not for our little wants and desires, but praying continually to be of service to God and to show a love for others.

College is a time when many Christians lose their faith or compromise in their morals. Why is this so? Well, some non-Christian scholars will try to act intelligent by saying something like: "The collegiate years are the times when young human minds are opened to all the knowledges of this world. They are no longer influenced by what their parents say is so. They reach the point where their minds no longer have to cave into the thoughts of a God to make them do good; they reach a new level of reason in which they see the ignorance of their childhood days." (taken from Dr. Stone's synopsis of his class given at orientation). But this could not be more false. Why many lose their faith is because they lack the closeness of God that they once had – they are out on their own and they find themselves not going to church, not reading their Bible, and being influence by a wave of sin that, more than likely, they have never seen before. There weak spiritual state allows Satan a golden opportunity to jump in and make these kids have doubts or disbelief. For I have never heard of anyone being discouraged from believing in God, when they were alive in Christ. There are no doubts in a person who loves and experiences God's goodness everyday. When

47

people give into sins or give into not believing in God, is when they are not close to Him and are not seeking His love.

Put yourself in Tony's position. Would you have the courage to share the good news about Jesus to 300 people you don't know? Would you have prayed like Tony everyday for the courage to stand up, or would you have done something like, drop the class or remain seating during the exam? Would you have the courage to stand up if a masked man with a gun came into a room and asked, "If you believe in God, stand up!"?

In your life, has there been times when you lacked the closeness to God that makes you want to do these things? Are you that close to Him right now?

When it comes to your life, are you the one sitting down letting others influence you, or are you the one who stands up and influences others?

Mark 11:22-24 Have faith in God," Jesus answered. "I tell you the truth, if anyone says to this mountain, `Go, throw yourself into the sea,' and does not doubt in his heart but believes that what he says will happen, it will be done for him. Therefore I tell you, whatever you ask for in prayer, believe that you have received it, and it will be yours.

Psalm 22:22 I will declare your name to my brothers; in the congregation I will praise you.

Luke 6:28 bless those who curse you, pray for those who mistreat you.

John 5:24 I tell you the truth, whoever hears my word and believes him who sent me has eternal life and will not be condemned; he has crossed over from death to life

Romans 14:22 I tell you the truth, whoever hears my word and believes him who sent me has eternal life and will not be condemned; he has crossed over from death to life

Romans 15:1 We who are strong ought to bear with the failings of the weak and not to please ourselves.

Hebrews 6:18 God did this so that, by two unchangeable things in which it is impossible for God to lie, we who have fled to take hold of the hope offered to us may be greatly encouraged.

The Unlikely Conversion

Tony Nichlaus (the freshman student whose story was in the previous tale, that stood up to his atheist philosophy teacher and converted many students to Christianity) was very pleased as to what God allowed him to do in class that day. But the young man still had compassion for Dr. Stone, even though he did say many awful things about God. Tony had finished his semester for that class and was not obligated to see the intimidating Dr. Stone again, but Tony wanted earnestly to help this man. Tony returned the next day to the empty lecture hall where Professor Stone was nowhere to be found, so Tony decided to leave a well-thought out note on his desk. The next day Professor Stone came across the note, which read:

"Dear Dr. Stone,

Of all the many hours you spoke to me about how God does not exist – I ask you to take 15 minutes out of your time to read of my past experiences with God, and attempt to answer the questions that I underlined after reading this letter.

I write to you because I once doubted in God, believed he was a waste of time – I was an atheist, but just not as outspoken as you. I viewed the preacher at my parent's church as a babbling idiot, an insular yahoo to say the least. At sixteen years old, I thought I had figured the world out, and I thought I knew everything. Until one day that preacher came up to me and told me the dumbest, childish story I've ever heard, but it is one I will never forget. It goes:

'There once was a frog that self-proclaimed himself king of a puddle of water along a path. One day he said out loud, "I am a mighty and great king; I know everything about my kingdom, and I rule over it with perfection." A dog was walking along the path and overheard the frog, so the dog asked the frog if the king would like to travel with him. The frog feeling honored agreed. The frog jumped up one the dog's back, and the dog took him to a beautiful pond. The frog's eyes sparkled at the sight of the body of water. The dog said to the King Frog, "Wait, there is more." Then the dog took the frog to a large lake, so large that the water stretched as far as the eye could see – the frog was now in disbelief. But the dog said, "you still have not seen it all yet." He then took the frog a little further down the path to the ocean. The frog's eyes nearly popped out of his head in excitement.'

This story showed me that I did not know everything. Like the frog, the more I explored into more areas of life, the more I found that I did not know.

I then got to know God by exploring the many forms of life, which in some way all led me to God. I never had the chance to share my faith with you until that last day. All the questions you asked us about God in class were all done in a philosophical way, and of course, none of us students could ever contradict you in these questions; you have a PH.D. in philosophy; we are only freshman and sophomores in college that have little or no experience in philosophy.

While you can explain all your philosophical questions, can you answer these five questions of mine?

1. <u>If there is no God, don't you think that all the millions of followers would figure out that they were wrong.</u> Look at the countless number of men that have spent their life studying scripture. Wouldn't these men who knew so much about God, be the ones to truly know if God was real or not. And while atheists have their theories on how things were created, they have less proof than what Christians have about God and the creation. Also, no atheist or someone from another religion can prove Christianity wrong.

2. In your lecture you criticized Christians for believing that the world was created 6,000 years ago, but nowhere in the Bible does it say that. And you said that it would be impossible to fit two or seven of each type of animal in Noah's arc – that there would not be enough room for 2 laboratory retrievers, 2 cocker spinals, 2 Great Danes, 2 poodles – but nowhere does it say that – it just says two or seven of each kind of animal. Even the theory of evolution, which you strongly hold onto permits for animals to change drastically over the years. <u>I've read the Bible over 4 times from front to back and have not found any mistakes; can you find any?</u>

3. My psychology professor tells us that we have not nearly figured out all about our brains, what our brain does, or what it is capable of. <u>If man cannot even fully understand his own brain, how can he truly understand that there is no God – a God that is much greater than a 4-pound organ?</u>

4. <u>Where did the world come from?</u> According to science, there is a cause that will produce an effect on everything (Newton's laws). For example, we have a sun from the cause of trillions of hydrogen atoms undergoing reactions causing the effect of lighting our world. But what was the cause that put the hydrogen atoms there. To me it is easier to believe in a God for the answer, instead of tracing everything in the universe back to an "uncaused cause" that no atheist can explain.

5. You can't know that God isn't real by reading books and thinking about it, because you do not know God by reading books - you know God by living with Him each day. That's why you do on have to be smart, rich, popular, beautiful, or wise to know God. That's why anyone can experience his love, and why they are willing to lay down their life for such a Thing. <u>So how can you prove God does not exists, when you do not even know Him?</u>

Professor Stone I hope you truly consider your choices in life, I will continue to pray for you.

May God be with you,

Tony Nichlaus"

Professor Stone crumbled up the letter as his face burned with anger. The thoughts of answers started to appear in his head, but he quickly realized that his answers were merely philosophical quotes that had no meaning and really did not answer the simple questions. He began to slowly straighten the balled up piece of paper, as the big 6'7' man began to break down in tears. He couldn't do it - a doctor in philosophy that had taught for twenty years, could not answer 5 simple questions asked by a nineteen year old boy.

He knew that his life he had lived was meaningless. He right then made a pact to God – the same God he taught against for 20 years.

The professor had to swallow his pride, and he tried to write to all his old students that he remained in contact with over the years. He told them that his life to that point was only good for an "example of a bad example."

The teacher that one day said, "whoever believes in God is a fool," now quotes Psalm 53:1 which says, "The fool says in his heart 'There is no God'."

Dr. Stone was able to turn his whole life around, and forget his thoughts that there was no God. Have you come to the point where you are 100% that there is a God, and He is worth ever bit of your time and effort here on earth? Do not bother yourself by trying to figure out God and why things on the earth are the way they are. Because no matter how smart you are, trying to figure these things out is like an ant trying to understand how an automobile works – it simply cannot be done. We must just have faith in God and his love will make His existence undeniable to us. When we believe 100% that He is God, then our life can truly be bound in his love.

Have you like Tony witnessed to individuals such as Professor Stone or someone that you think would never receive the gospel. Never underestimate how God works. Through my experiences of ministering to others, some of the ones that do receive Christ are the ones that I never would have expected. Why some people do bad

53

things or curse God is because they do not have any love in their life. When they see the love of a Christian that is reaching out to them and, most importantly, the love of God that cares for them, this love changes them into a different person.

Ask yourself, could you prove Jesus is Lord to a nonbeliever? Could you ask the questions to point an atheist to God? If you met a man like Professor Stone would his teachings make you think long and hard about God, or would your faith force him to think long and hard about God.

Be assertive in knowing God as Creator of this Universe, and show your love, so you may be an example to all that he is real. By doing so, your life will be resting in God's loving hands.

John 14:1 Do not let your hearts be troubled. Trust in God; trust also in me.

1 John 3:23 And this is his command: to believe in the name of his Son, Jesus Christ, and to love one another as he commanded us.

Isaiah 40:28 Do you not know? Have you not heard? The LORD is the everlasting God, the Creator of the ends of the earth.

Isaiah 44:6 This is what the LORD says— Israel's King and Redeemer, the LORD Almighty:

I am the first and I am the last; apart from me there is no God.

Acts 10:42 He commanded us to preach to the people and to testify that he is the one whom God appointed as judge of the living and the dead.

2 Timothy 4:2 Preach the Word; be prepared in season and out of season; correct, rebuke and encourage—with great patience and careful instruction.

2 Timothy 1:12 That is why I am suffering as I am. Yet I am not ashamed, because I know whom I have believed, and am convinced that he is able to guard what I have entrusted to him for that day

Little Wings flying us to Heaven

Alison Malone was a beautiful 12-year old girl from Baton Rouge, Louisiana. Her bright, blue eyes and curly blond her gave her the nickname "Goldie Lox." However, her beautiful outward appearance only masked the pain inside, for her father Dan Malone was a ragging alcoholic. While sober, Dan seemed to be a well-mannered man; however, after drinking, Dan's violent side came out of him. He would usually return home where bitter arguments erupted between him and his wife. Unfortunately, Dan would take out his anger from those arguments on his wife and young Alison. Under Alison's flowery dresses and long curly hair, were many bumps and bruised that bore the marks of her father's abuse. When Alison's father would barge home from drinking, Alison would run upstairs to her room and close the door. She could still hear the yelling and commotion downstairs, but she would curl up into a corner, say a prayer, and grew, as she called it, "wings" that flew her up to heaven and away from the violence at her house. She would return to school the next day keeping quiet about the cause of the bumps and bruises, and she would say nothing about what happened the night before. Because of all of the great trials put in front of her, Alison only found one place of comfort and that was at her grandmother's house where she read Bible stories, sleep at peace in her grandmother's bed, and was around someone that loved her.

Late one cold, February night, Dan stormed home after being away from his family for several days. Alison was not too excited to see her missing father. She knew through his aggressive entry and violent stare that her father had been drinking. Alison quickly ran to her room, sat in her corner, and prayed, "Dear God, Please be in this house tonight. Please let daddy not do anything to hurt me or Mommy. Make Daddy be nice and not so mad. Let me fly away from here, and be where you are. Please God."

Alison would put on her wings and fly to heaven for the last time that night. For the alcohol got too much of Dan, and it made him accidentally take away his innocent daughter's life. At least now, Alison has the comfort in heaven that she prayed for. She is where there will never be another beating, where no more tears will be cried in that corner, and where she will no longer have to grow "wings" to get her to heaven, for Alison is now resting up under God's comforting hand.

When fear overtakes you, do you go to God for comfort?

When stress controls your life, do you go to God for help?

When pain hurts you, do you go to God for relief?

When uncertainty overtakes you, do you go to God for reassurance?

When you have had enough of this world, do you grow "wings" and fly to heaven?

Living in this world, we will see some pretty awful things; we will experience some rough times; and we will realize we live in a wicked, cruel world. However, for us Christians, we have the assurance that we are just living here: our home is in heaven.

Our days will come and go, as will periods of good and periods of bad, but it is only time that separates us from our true home: our home that Alison wished to be at, the home we long for, the home where everything is perfect.

The evil that we face and the pain that we go through will only make heaven seem that much more wonderful to us. We cannot change the world we live in, but we can live in a different world than where we are at now. We can always have the hope of God in our lives; when times get too rough, we can always grow "wings" to fly us to heaven. God will be there to be a Rock of Refuge, Comforter, Redeemer, and Friend. Every moment of everyday, he wants to be the one that is there for you when you are hurting. We may have to suffer insults, beatings, loneliness, depression, and constant pain; but no one is deprived of God's love.

We were not made to be happy in a world of hate, evil, and despair; but we were made to be with God, who gives us joy even through life's worst times.

I John 3:2 Dear friends, now we are children of God, and what we will be has not yet been made known. But we know that when he appears, we shall be like him, for we shall see him as he is. Everyone who has this hope in him purifies himself, just as he is pure.

Psalm 19:14 May the words of my mouth and the meditation of my heart be pleasing in your sight, O LORD, my Rock and my Redeemer

Psalm 25:14 The LORD confides in those who fear him; he makes his covenant known to them.

Psalm 78:35 They remembered that God was their Rock, that God Most High was their Redeemer.

Isaiah 44:6 This is what the LORD says— Israel's King and Redeemer, the LORD Almighty:

I am the first and I am the last; apart from me there is no God.

Revelation 7:17 For the Lamb at the center of the throne will be their shepherd; he will lead them to springs of living water. And God will wipe away every tear from their eyes."

A Change of Heart

Dan Malone was sentenced to 50 years in prison for child abuse, which resulted in his little girl, Alison's death (this was the story in the last devotional). In prison, Dan the ragging alcoholic obviously had to sober up, and when he sobered up, he began to think with a right mind. A local pastor came and told Dan of his little girl's story and how she found God as her comfort. It was then when it fully sunk in as to what he had done, and Dan finally saw himself as the monster that he had turned into. Right then, Dan decided to change his life, and through several visits from the pastor, Dan learned that God still loved him even for the evil creature he was. Dan was a changed man. He would go on to only serve 25 years of his 50-year sentence due to his good behavior, and he is now traveling the country with his wife (that he once abused) speaking to young adults about the harms of alcohol and how God delivered him from the life he once lived.

The Heberts were known around the small town of Sawgrass, Arkansas as the rudest, meanest, toughest, and evil family around. Bobby Hebert, like the rest of his family, got into trouble at a young age. Through his teenage years, Bobby was caught smoking, drinking, stealing and doing many other crimes. By the age of 18, Bobby dropped out of high school, and joined a rock band in which he was the lead guitarist. The band would travel all across the state, while all of its members were involved in drugs, sex, and other things that Bobby now says "people could not even imagine." At 23, he laid in the hospital bed half dead from a drug overdose. It was then that one of his friends from a bar that he did gigs at, came to him telling of the greatness of Jesus and how He could get him out of this situation. But Bobby only got angry and furiously said, "I'm Bobby Hebert, I don't go to anybody for help." A month later, Bobby returned to that friend and wanted help. He would go on to find the Lord that day. Bobby found his life no longer filled with sin and emptiness, but it was now filled with the greatness of God. Today, Bobby is a missionary in Japan with his wife (the girl from the bar that led him to Christ), where he plays his guitar to a different tune for hundreds of Japanese children waiting to praise God.

C.S. Lewis, one of the greatest Christian writers of all-time, spent almost ½ of his life as a devout atheist.

Saul persecuted hundreds of Christians, even killing his hated foe, before he was converted to the Paul of the Bible that we know today.

These men were cruel, evil, and hated God, but that did not stop God from coming into their lives. God not only turned their life completely around, but also he turned them into: a evangelistic speaker who has warned thousands of teenagers and adults about the dangers of alcohol; a missionary that preaches the gospel and leads worship for thousands in Japan; a writer that has had more of an impact on believers than anyone of the last century; and an apostle and writer of a large part of the Bible.

These men's stories remind me of a lesson in chemistry class when you take one thing and react it to another, so that it becomes an entirely different thing. For example, you can take sodium, a very reactive earth metal (so reactive it usually gives off an explosion or loud pop when it comes is contact with something like water). Then take chlorine (which is so poisonous in its pure gas form that just smelling traces of it would kill a human being). And put these two dangerous elements together, you get… table salt, something we use everyday.

God is the key ingredient that turns our life from whatever sin and Satan has done with it, to a harmless compound that will only get better with age. There are so many stories out there of the "bad" one, the prisoner, the ex-drug addict, the atheist, and the one we picture in hell that ends up becoming a new creature and accepting faith in God.

First ask yourself, do you completely have that key ingredient that turns you from deserving the worst punishment of hell, to having the paradise of heaven.

Then, make sure that you find yourself not being judgmental. You can look at a person and see that they live a bad life, which makes you think less of them, and you never try to reach out to that person. However, that person is just as worthy of God's grace as anybody else. For even Jesus tells us that the one who has the greatest debt forgiven, will be thankful the most. So, do not turn up your nose or fail to witness to anybody for what they have done or for what kind of person they are, because they can be a child of God just like you.

Never forget that nothing is impossible with God. In these four circumstances, nobody would have given these men a chance into becoming what they became. So why can't your life also be turned around in such a way? The only thing that got them there was God, and don't you also have this ingredient in your life?

Who is someone that is hard to picture as a Christian that you could reach out to this week?

Over his years a man will change, but only God can change a man's heart.

Ezekiel 33:11 As surely as I live, declares the Sovereign LORD, I take no pleasure in the death of the wicked, but rather that they turn from their ways and live. Turn! Turn from your evil ways! Why will you die, O house of Israel?'

Acts 3:19-21 Repent, then, and turn to God, so that your sins may be wiped out, that times of refreshing may come from the Lord,

Acts 17:30 In the past God overlooked such ignorance, but now he commands all people everywhere to repent

Acts 26:20b First to those in Damascus, then to those in Jerusalem and in all Judea, and to the Gentiles also, I preached that they should repent and turn to God and prove their repentance by their deeds

Serving others

Jason Thompson was an 18 year-old kid that just graduated high school in Memphis, Tennessee. Jason wanted more than anything to serve God by becoming a missionary. While he wanted to get a formal education in religion at a university, he knew that this could wait, for he felt God was calling Him to be a missionary first. Jason went to Victory Outreach & Missionary Ministry in his hometown looking for a way to get into the mission field. The group, seeing two hands willing to work, allowed him to join a team going to central Africa. They sat Jason down and warned him that this was no week long trip that you take with a Church youth group, but this was a dangerous 6-month undertaking, where they would witness to people who never have seen a white man or heard the gospel. There could even be a chance of death from these natives, wild animals, or disease. Without hesitation, Jason said that this was exactly what he wanted to do, and he signed up.

Over in Africa, the first couple weeks did not go as planned for Jason. Since he did not have a college degree, adequate missionary training, or know the native tongue, Jason was assigned the small tasks that did not involve ministry. For example, he had the jobs of going to the well to get water, finding scrap wood for building things, cooking meals, and helping doctors care for the sick/injured. However, Jason never got discouraged; he prayed to God that he would be of use; and he did everything no matter how small the task with great effort.

Things would get better – he would meet friendly natives at the well and bring them back to camp for the other missionaries to witness to; he was picking up on the language of the region while attending to the sick/injured; and he was able to establish a great friendship with the children by playing games and interacting with them. Six months flew by, and Jason was not ready to leave. He figured he already missed ½ of a year of college what was another six months? So he came home for Christmas where he was welcomed by his family and members of his church. In fact, one of those church members surprised Jason by offering to sponsor Jason's trip back to Africa and pay for his fees for as many years as Jason wanted to be a missionary.

Upon returning back to Africa, Jason received a nice reception by all the children that he had been ministering to. He brought each one of them a little toy from home, and each one of them thanked him with a hug and bright smile on their face - Jason knew that this was his true calling. Even though, he was not the one preaching the Word or praying with the children to receive Christ, he was having such an impact by serving in little ways.

Time would go on and to this day, Jason Thompson, now 44 years of age, is still ministering in Central Africa. It took him a little over two and a half years to learn the language good enough to communicate with the people, but since then, he has not stopped telling the Good News to all in the region. He has led thousands to Christ, and it is not because he is a gifted speaker – because he never received a college education, never attended seminary, never went through a missionary training course, and is no more naturally talented in speaking than the next guy. But why Jason has had such an impact, is because he has always been willing to serve. Even though he preaches a good deal, he spends twice as much time doing what he did when he first got there – the small tasks. He has helped give treatment to thousands of AIDS patients, built many homes for the homeless, and has ministered to a countless number of children which he helps raise growing up in the Lord.

Jason Thompson and his mission ministry is an awesome example of servant hood.

Think about this: when Jesus came down to earth, He did not act like the King of the universe like He is, but He came to serve.

We have the meaning of being successful and influential all mixed up. It's not the amount of people that are serving us that makes us influential, it is the opposite – it's how many we serve. For example, we think of the most influential pastors are the ones that have the most people in their church attendance. Or we think of most successful businessmen as the ones that have the big office with a huge window overlooking the city. But God has proven through countless times in the Bible, that numbers or size does not mean a thing. Like in Jason's situation, he never was the best speaking preacher, and he usually preached to a group of natives less than ten; but he had a great impact because he was willing to serve.

The great thing about serving is that everybody can do it. All you need is a willing attitude and a lot of effort.

What makes a great servant is how readily one is to serve. Very few people go the extra step having this willingness to serve all the time. I know, for me, I struggle a good deal in this area. Sure, I will put in a good effort serving for others in volunteer/community service during the times I commit myself to these things, but I find myself serving little during the other times on my schedule. It is easy to serve when I have devoted a block of time, for say, something like community service, but what about the times like when I am going to the movies and see someone broken down on the side of the road. Would missing the previews be that big of a deal?

One of the greatest ways to show love is to serve others; just think about it - are we not loving others as ourselves when we serve?

So many of us find ourselves serving in some way; however, just not serving all the time.

Being a servant, one does not thinking about himself. Everything is done strictly for the benefit of others, not for the benefits of yourself. Too many people expect that if they serve that it will bring something good to them. They think: "God will bless me more for doing extra," "others will recognized/praised my efforts," or "this will sound good for me on a resume or when I discuss it with others." However, a true servant is concerned for only those he serves; a true servant serves from the heart.

God would rather us be a servant than being a leader.

He would rather you humbly help out unfortunate others, than trying to make your life great.

He would rather you give your time doing a few little things for another, than trying to do many things with your life.

He would rather you serve, than to be something great.

How have you in your life served others or the kingdom of God?

Do others think of you as a servant?

Never forget how much serving others will change the world.

Philippians 2:5 -7 Your attitude should be the same as that of Christ Jesus: Who, being in very nature God, did not consider equality with God something to be grasped but made himself nothing, taking the very nature of a servant, being made in human likeness

Mark 10:43 Not so with you. Instead, whoever wants to become great among you must be your servant,

Luke 4:8 Jesus answered, "It is written: 'Worship the Lord your God and serve him only

John 12:26 Whoever serves me must follow me; and where I am, my servant also will be. My Father will honor the one who serves me.

Corinthians 12:5 There are different kinds of service, but the same Lord. There are different kinds of working, but the same God works all of them in all men

Seeking Pleasure

Brevie Berkson was the lead singer and songwriter for a rock and roll band from Monica, England. Like many other British icons before him, Brevie would accomplish worldwide fame with his singing. His albums sold millions, his concerts were sold out, and the paparazzi took pictures of him wherever he went. Brevie would also follow the rock stars before him by living a life of indulging in pleasure.

Since he had money rolling in, Brevie spent millions for all the luxuries in life. First came the expensive cars and the large mansion. Then this was not good enough, so he had to have everything in his car and house to be top-notch (even his toilet seat was covered in 24 ct. gold, costing well over ½ million dollars.) Then one house was no longer good enough, so he bought places all around the globe. However after a short time, all the things money could buy was not good enough. So then he moved on to women. Groupies followed this rock and roll icon everywhere, so Brevie would pleasure himself by doing whatever he wanted sexually with any girl he choose. When one girl was no longer good enough, he would have two, when two was not good enough, then he would chose several to spend the night. After some time, Brevie no longer found pleasure in this, for every night would be the same thing just with a different woman - he was not satisfied. He blamed his problem on his sexuality and made amends by calling himself a homosexual. So he tried to find pleasure in this road of life, but it was not long that Brevie discovered that this too was not sufficient. He then turned to drugs to fill the void in his life. He started "small" by using marijuana and alcohol, but soon they would no longer satisfied him. He would eventually take the serious stuff like cocaine and heroin. Even though these drugs made him feel different feelings, they were not the feeling that he was searching for – they too left him unsatisfied. Brevie Berkson had everything – he had millions of dollars, the greatest mansions, the coolest cars, thousand of women willing to do anything for him, fame known worldwide, and at the youthful age of 26 he had his whole life to do whatever he wanted. He had the perfect life didn't he?

Well, Brevie did not agree. Late one night after a concert he could not take it anymore. He got a pen and wrote on a napkin:

"The Same, the same, the same
Life is all the same
The money, sex, and fame
It is all the same, all the same,

People spend their lives wanting it
Others spend all their life to finally get it
I have spent my whole life having it
But it's all the same; It's all the same

Man lives only to the return to the dust in which he came
Having it all, having all he wants is his chief aim
Between from dust to dust man searches for this one thing
That being having all the same, having all the same.

Though our dreams may not be the same
The satisfaction from them are all the same

67

This world is all the same
All the same, all the same."

Then underneath these lyrics he writes:
"The same, the same, the same,
I can no longer live this life of same"

Brevie then took out a pistol, stuck it in his mouth and pulled the trigger.

Brevie had everything, but had nothing.

Did you see the pattern in Brevie's life? Can you see how the pursuit of pleasure is meaningless? The pursuit of pleasure is all the same.

Isn't odd that most people would want to have Brevie's life more than their own? But why? What did he have that brings pleasure to Him that does not bring pleasure to your life?
So many of us seek pleasure by wanting and trying the different things of life, but we are never satisfied.

Pleasure gives us joy for a second, but the next second we are left wanting more. Like Brevie, we keep wanting more – there is never satisfaction from the things of this world.
For the endless pleasure seeking to stop, we must seek God who truly satisfies our longings. God is that which satisfies us.
God designed pleasure in a certain way – a way that will leave us wanting more; the more only God can provide. All our longings are from a hole in our heart. We can try to fit pleasures in this hole, but they soon will escape. However with God, we find that He is the perfect fit for this hole – now with this complete heart, our lives can be complete. We no longer seek pleasure, but pleasure can be found in everything.

Pleasure is rooted up in us too much. It seems to be the benchmark to which we judge things – if it does not bring fun, it is no good. Everyone sets this standard in some way. When someone asked me, "How was the mission trip?" I replied, "I loved it, it was fun." Not "the Lord greatly used me," or "I learned many things about God" but "It was fun." Indicating it was good because it was fun. Having fun or pleasure should not be a standard or benchmark in which we judge life. For if we use pleasure as a benchmark in Brevie's life, it would be great; however, we know otherwise.

The sin of pleasure is like a computer virus. Somehow the virus will get into our computer. Our computer will then receive the virus before it receives vital data and operates key functions. As it makes its way in the computer, it makes the computer do what it is not supposed to do. It then leaves itself empty and if not taken out it will cause harm. The sins of pleasure, too, will pop up in our lives though some temptation. We then will take part in this pleasure before doing what we are supposed to do. Then afterwards the pleasure leaves itself empty, and if not taken out, will cause harm.

You can try to find happiness in the world though various sins, but aren't you looking for the pleasure that only comes from God?

Matthew 26:41 Watch and pray so that you will not fall into temptation. The spirit is willing, but the body is weak."

Ecclesiastes 2:1 I thought in my heart, "Come now, I will test you with pleasure to find out what is good." But that also proved to be meaningless.

Ecclesiastes 7:29 This only have I found: God made mankind upright, but men have gone in search of many schemes

Proverbs 21:17a He who loves pleasure will become poor;

Hebrews 13:18b We are sure that we have a clear conscience and desire to live honorably in every way

2 Peter 2:13-14a, 17 They will be paid back with harm for the harm they have done. Their idea of pleasure is to carouse in broad daylight. They are blots and blemishes, reveling in their pleasures while they feast with you. With eyes full of adultery, they never stop sinning.

These men are springs without water and mists driven by a storm. Blackest darkness is reserved for them.

1 John 4:4 You, dear children, are from God and have overcome them, because the one who is in you is greater than the one who is in the world.

The Power of Prayer

Rebecca Howell was a 16-year-old girl who worked at Central Park in New York City selling lemonade. On the Fourth of July, Rebecca was required to work late because of a firework show that night. Rebecca was not used to walking back home in the dark, and there was just something that seemed to scare her that night. On the way home, Rebecca had a choice to take a shortcut through an alley, which was scary even in the daytime, or take the three extra blocks to get to her house. Being very anxious to get back home, she decided to take the abandoned alley. As she walked, the alley became pitch dark; she grew terribly frightened; and she knew that she made a bad choice. She could hear voices but could not see faces. She quickened her paced. Her hands were shaking. And fear had overtaken her. At that moment, she began praying to God with tears streaming down her cheeks, "God I pray that you would at this moment allow me to get to safety this night. I feel so helpless and defenseless right now, and I pray that you would be my strength. I am praying to you know because I know that no one else besides you could deliver me from harm if someone wanted to hurt me; God I pray that you would be right by my side this very moment. As she ended her prayer, she ran into an evil-looking man that was staring right in her eyes. The light was only visible to see his face. Rebecca was stunned; she stood motionless. She finally caught her senses and began to run the rest of the way home untouched. The next morning, Rebecca heard of news that a girl had been raped in the same alley that she had went through the night before. Rebecca went to the authorities to tell the police that she had walk down that alley, just minutes before the crime was committed. The police then asked her to go look at a line up of several men and to see if any looked familiar. One man jumped out - it was the man that she stared in the eye the night before; it was a face that she never would forget. The police thanked her, saying that she only supported the evidence that was given by the other girl. Rebecca asked the policeman if she could ask the criminal just one question, and the officer agreed. So Rebecca looked the man in the eye and said, "Why wasn't it me that you attacked last night?" The man said, "Because I saw two large men standing by your side"

This story is an excellent example of the power of prayer. Prayer is a powerful thing that is very important in our lives; however, most of us never utilize it.

Communication and language is a defining part of humans – something no animal can mimic. Being able to communicate is one of the human's main goals – this is why we get so excited in hearing an infant's first word. Today, communication is everywhere between everyone. Whether it is talking in the midst of friends, through cell phones, over the Internet, or through television, we are communicating in some way.

So why do fail to communicate to God through prayer? Could you imagine not be able to talk or communicate at all to someone you loved? Could you have a dating relationship with someone if you never talk to them? So why don't we talk to God?

Many times we grow confused and think God does not want to listen, and He will not care enough to provide what we ask for. But God loves us, and like it would be hard for a father to say no to his little boy who says, "please Daddy- I love you," so too it would hard for God to say no to us.

This reminds me of a story that a pastor told in his sermon that said,

"A Christian man once died and went to heaven, and an angel took him to a large warehouse. On the way they passed many mansions; the man grew anxious for he thought of which one of these mansions would be the one that Jesus had promised to him. But the angel took him to a large, ugly warehouse. Inside the warehouse were boxes and boxes so numerous to count, and the angel said, "Inside all these boxes are your gifts" The man stood in amazement and said,"all this mine!" "No" said the angel. You will have all that you need now that you are in heaven; all of this is what you could have had - I was just showing you your gifts that you could have been given to you on earth. And it would have been given to you, if you only asked." The man fell upon his face and said, "I wanted these gifts, but I thought that I had to do everything myself. I needed the gifts, but I did not know how to get them. I thought God didn't care or didn't have an answer."

So whatever it is that you wish God to do or whatever troubles you – don't be afraid to take it to God in prayer. There are so many gifts that God has to give and so many situations that God can get you out of – all you need to do is pray to God that these gifts will be given unto you.

Today I would like to end with something a little different. Instead of saying a normal prayer I would encourage you to recite the famous Prayer of Jabez. It is a powerful prayer that asks you to overcome and be blessed. I ask you to dwell on these words and say them with all you heart:

"Oh, that you would bless me and enlarge my territory! Let your hand be with me, and keep me from harm so that I will be free from pain."
(1 Chronicles 4:10)

Philippians 4:6 Do not be anxious about anything, but in everything, by prayer and petition, with thanksgiving, present your requests to God.

Nick Shelton

1 John 5:14 This is the confidence we have in approaching God: that if we ask anything according to his will, he hears us. And if we know that he hears us—whatever we ask—we know that we have what we asked of him

Matthew 21:22 If you believe, you will receive whatever you ask for in prayer."

James 5:13,15 Is any one of you in trouble? He should pray. Is anyone happy? Let him sing songs of praise. the prayer offered in faith will make the sick person well; the Lord will raise him up. If he has sinned, he And will be forgiven.

Greek Pride

Aerocles was a powerful king of ancient Greece that ruled the city-state Pelocees. While Pelocees was not as populated as Troy, as powerful of a military force as Sparta, or as wealthy as Athens, it was a fine coastal city that boasted great fishing and marvelous shipbuilding. However over the years, Aerocles was able to transform his small city-state into a major power in the country. The astute king was able to collect vast amounts of wealth by selling the world-famous Pelocean ships/boats across the known world. Because the Pelocean people were very peaceful and Aerocles was such a good man, many kings and nobility were willing to do business with him. Since Aerocles did not go out to conquer other nations and Pelocees was on a protected, secluded spot on the peninsula, the Pelocean people did not fight many wars; thus, allowing its population to grow larger and larger.

As the city grew stronger and stronger over the years, King Aerocles became more and more prideful. Although his riches at his palace and estates were far plenty, Aerocles wanted more. On the famous Pelocean ships, Aerocles would send his men all over the Mediterranean, especially to the African continent, to loot small cities and to take captives. Aerocles' men brought back gold, rubies, and even diamonds from far away; plus, they would capture many men that were skilled fighters that would greatly aid to Aerocles's army. One of the captives, named Gratha, Aerocles was especially proud. Gratha was a seven-foot giant from an African country. He had muscles that bulged from his body; his armor weighed more than a typical man; and he could throw a spear a good 50 feet farther than any other warrior. With his great army and many riches, Aerocles let pride sink in, and he no longer sold his ships to other kingdoms. Before, Aerocles was much loved by neighboring city-states and countries, but now he was becoming a hated tyrant. Even though all other kings were just as prideful or just as power-hungry, the similar bond of pride made them detest one another.

Aerocles wanted more - he wanted to be remembered as a great king who had vast amounts of wealth and had taken over much land. Aerocles would expand his territory by conquering the nearby city-states and other weak territories.

One day, the king from Athens asked Aerocles to allow his army to use some Pelocean ships and warriors to help in an Athenian victory against a warring nation to the north (in Greek custom this would have shown that the king of Athens thought to be superior to Aerocles). Aerocles was appalled, and he exclaimed, "Who is this king to ask me for my ships and my men." Furiously, he would send off the Athenian messengers to tell the king of Athens, "I could take over your city with my men, and you would see how much more of a superior state that we are than you." The Athenian king took this as a major threat and challenged Aerocles to bring his men and try to take the city. While this was not what Aerocles meant when he angrily sent off the Athenian messengers, his pride would not let him back down from the king's challenge. So Aerocles and his men, went up to Athens prepared to fight. Aerocles wanted for the battle to be fought against the two most powerful warriors, with Pelocees sending out Gratha. But the Athenian king said that if it was going to be a fight for the city, then all of the city's army would fight. So for a weeklong period, the two armies fought. The Athenians decimated the Pelocean army and killed Aerocles. The Athenian warriors went down to Pelocees, ransacked the city, stole all of its treasures, and loaded them all up on the Pelocean ships that they likewise stole to sail back home.

And just like that Aerocles' great and might city-state was destroyed by his own pride, and Pelocees was like a mighty wave that ceased to exist, as it crashed upon the shore.

Pride can be the most harmful of all sins. It is also the oldest sin. Satan's pride cast him away from being with God. Pride was the reason sin came into mankind, when Adam and Eve ate of the fruit hoping to become like God.

Pride is the opposite of what the Christian life stands for. It is the opposite of love.

Pride destroys our character and our ability to love. As Christians when we become prideful, we think more and more of ourselves, we no longer feel that we need Jesus for our sins, and from this point, Satan is in control to do whatever he wants to do in our lives.

We as Christians have all had it in our lives. Some point down the road, we begin to think of ourselves as a good person. We think we are doing so good as a Christian, since we do not sin as much as we used to. We compare ourselves to others, and we see ourselves as better than most people, so we begin to think more highly of ourselves.

But no matter how much good you have done or how many sins you avoided, you are still in dire dependence on God's grace. This dependence on God is what allows for spiritual growth and coming closer to God. This is why pride can be such a destructive force in you life.

Pride is so apparent in our culture, and it is mainly apparent through money. For we see it all the time, men spend their lives and even degrade their morals to get more. It is not as though they need the money to support themselves/family; they want it because they want the pride of having more. Money has become symbolic for power in our day. People find themselves becoming just like Aerocles with his pride for power with our pride for money.

It does not take much pride to corrupt our thinking, and when our thoughts change, so do our actions. And these actions (like in Aerocles' case) will lead us to ruin. So how do we be un-prideful or modest? As for Aerocles case, he did not have to sink into everyone's demands. He did not have to go around saying to the other kings, "your city-state is much better than mine." But for Aerocles to be humble, all he had to do, was to listen to others, allow others to buy his ships, and treat everyone of his countrymen and enemies with respect. The same is true in our lives; we do not have to go around praising others all the time, but to be humble we must "treat others as ourselves."

Pride not only destroys our character and how we act as Christians, but it also destroys how others look at us. Pride is odd because it is something that is disliked by all. As C.S. Lewis points out, men who engage in sins like debauchery, stealing, sexual immorality, etc., usually get along great with other men who likewise do the same sin. However, a prideful man never gets along with another prideful man (like in the case of Aerocles and the other kings).[1]

How much pride do you have in your life?
The only pride we should have is - that we are a part of God's creation and a part of his family. This is the only pride that should be visible in our lives.

Romans 12:3,16 For by the grace given me I say to every one of you: Do not think of yourself more highly than you ought, but rather think of yourself with sober judgment, in accordance with the measure of faith God has given you.
Live in harmony with one another. Do not be proud, but be willing to associate with people of low position. Do not be conceited.

Deuteronomy 8:14 then your heart will become proud and you will forget the LORD your God, who brought you out of Egypt, out of the land of slavery.
Proverbs 11:2 When pride comes, then comes disgrace, but with humility comes wisdom.
Proverbs 16:18 Pride goes before destruction, a haughty spirit before a fall.

[1] Source: Mere Christianity, C.S. Lewis

When Satan Attacks

The Devil was out roaming the earth, recruiting as many humans as he could to join his band in Hell. He headed up north to Boston, MA where he was going to talk strategy with one of his fallen angels, Demon #8. The two went in disguise into a local restaurant. The Devil said, "You know #8, there's a lot of people in this world that has not discovered the meaning of life. They are living the journey of life walking down a tightrope. Instead of letting them reach the other side, God's side, we must shake their rope, or let a little wind come in their direction, or just push them off, making them fall straight down to Hell in our hands.

"Take for instance that young man over there," as the Devil eyed a tall, muscular man that stood a head taller than the rest of the crowd. "That man was a famous basketball star. He was drafted into the NBA after two years of college. He immediately gained a life of fame and riches, and he was living the life of his dreams. However, two years ago, he had a serious knee injury, and he has not played since. The money and the fame left him quicker than you can say, "Holy Smokes." He will live the rest of his life miserable because he does not have the things that he used to. That is, as long as we can keep him seeking after the things he once had, rather than seeking after God.

"And look over their," the Devil was now pointing to a young man with glasses. "That guy is smart. He scored a perfect score on his SAT college entrance exam; he has an exceptional I.Q., and graduated Harvard with a 4.0 G.P.A. He thinks he knows it all. He is a nuclear physicist that can explain how, what, why, and where everything happened. And you know what we do to this guy #8? – We use his strength, his own brain against him. We get him in such deep thought about God that he will prove to himself that God is not real, and that He is only a waste of time for someone as smart as himself.

"Who's that over there?" asked #8 pointing to a man with an expensive business suit and leather briefcase.

"That's Morgan McMicheal, business conglomerate and multi-millionaire; he is about the richest man in Boston. He is one of the best businessmen in history; he knows how to make money. But he is always wanting more. As long as we keep him wanting more, we have him right where we want him #8."

The Devil then turned his attention to a beautiful young girl that was with her boyfriend. "That girl seems to be a good gal. She is always known for being the 'nice one,' you know the one that is always polite, the one that cannot get angry, the one that goes out of her way to make others happy, you know the type."

Demon #8 responded, "Yeah, but isn't that what God wants these creatures to be like?"

"Well sort of, but this individual never came to God. So all of her good work will be useless. We must keep her busy of doing 'good,' and not doing things for God."

"On the other hand, that man has heard the work of God's plan. But he has seen so many Christians do so many bad things, he rationalizes that he is not such a bad guy. So he follows by no rules and does whatever he wants in his life. So all we have to do, #8, is keep letting him think that he is a 'good' person that is better than everybody else, and he will be right where we want him."

"The man beside him is a man that is consumed over sexual sins. The Lord blessed this man with a good deal of testosterone, so we must bless him with a good deal of temptations to tempt his sexual desire. We must not only tempt him, but we make him think that his sin is right because it feels right. We make him think that since it is so difficult for him to resist these temptations; that it is only natural to give into these sins. When we get someone like him attached to a sin and thinking he is doing nothing wrong, then he will not follow God; for he will not readily give up this sin."

#8 then pointed to a teenage girl crying at a table. "What about her, she looks like an easy target. How do we tempt her?"

The Devil shook his head and said, "your wrong on that one. That's a girl whose mother died when she was 12 leaving behind her, her dad, and 7 other brothers and sisters. She and her father work all day at minimum way jobs to support the family. You would think she would be more vulnerable to our attacks than anybody else, but that's not the case. She has God in her life, and she could not be a bit happier. She's crying because she just lost her job as a waitress at this restaurant, but she will find another one; it will probably be minimum wage, but she will be still be content. She's different. Even though she does not have possessions, she has love. Kind like hers are hard to break, but we will always have our fair share of humans under our control #8."

Satan is a real figure, and he does attack/tempt us everyday. He may not go to a restaurant with one of his demons to plot our downfall, but he knows our weakness and strategies to lead us astray. He attacks our thoughts and puts things in front of us to tempt us into doing wrong. One does not realize in how many ways Satan attack our minds.

Here are some of the many ways Satan attacks our thoughts:

- One of his main attacks is that Satan makes us feel useless. Our useless feeling leads to depression, which leads to one not being able to function at their best ability; and we eventually get to the point where we don't even try. We must recognize how much God loves us no matter what we have done. As long as we abide in this love, this attitude of being worthless should avoid us.
- Another main attack that Satan uses is making us think that we are good and do a lot of good things. He wants us to look

at others and think that we are a better person than they are. When he gets us with this attitude, we feel that we do not need God in our lives. Although we are just as much of a sinner as everyone else, we do not go to God for forgiveness and do not come to worship him with a humble heart. That person's life becomes more like the egotistical Pharisee, instead of a Christian whose heart seeks God's love. Everyone of us, even the most devout Christian, must be constantly reminded that we are "filthy rags" and full of sin.

- Satan also uses the trick of making us think that life is passing us by when we commit ourselves to God. He makes us think, "I only have one chance to live in this world, so why not do what is fun and desirable." He even goes to the extent of telling us that we are saved by grace, so that we can do anything we want and still be forgiven. But if we cave into these things, we not only sin, but more importantly, we take a step toward Satan. Each step we take the farther we get in. The farther we get in, the harder it is to get out. We must remember that though we may love to have fun, fun does not bring us love. Doing what is desirable is not the same as doing what brings joy.

- Satan wants us to desire to be someone different. He wants us to want to be like that movie actor, like that person who is attractive, or like that cool friend. When we really want to be like these people, we try to become like these individual instead of becoming the individual God wants us to be. Jesus should be our role model before anyone else.

- Satan also uses the strategy of preventing us from seeing what is really going on around us. He wants us to always be busy and chasing after things (they even may be good things), so that we do not get a chance to see where our life is heading. When we get wrapped up in all the things of the world, he can slowly draw us farther and farther away from God, until we get to the point when it is nothing for us to go against Him. In order to stop him, we should be constantly having a "check up" and examine where we are going in our life and how we are growing in the Lord.

- Another way Satan attempts to lead us astray is making us see everything in the world from a self-centered way. He wants us to see our friend get married, and instead of being happy for him/her, he wants to make us think that we must fall in love. He wants us to see a co-worker who just ran a marathon, and instead of admiring what he did, he wants us to think that we must do something else impressive to show him up. He wants us to see our neighbor drive into their driveway with a new car, and he wants us to desire having a better one. We should remember that everything in our life should be centered on God and not our selves.

- Satan also uses the technique of trying to mix us up in what is right and what we think is right. There are so many ways he can do this (like how I mentioned when the prideful man thinks he is always doing good). He can also get us to do what feels right; instead of, doing what we know is right. He will give us many excuses on how a certain sin can be good and have good consequences. But, we must study scripture, know what is right, and not turn from what the Bible says.

And there are so many other ways Satan tempts us in our lives. He is not merely a red creature with horns and a pitchfork that sits on our shoulder telling us to do bad. He is a deceiver; he leads us astray without us ever knowing it.

So how can we prevent his attacks? We must find ways to resist the Devil (I will discuss this more in detail in the next devotion). The best attack against the devil is knowing God and living a life of love.

I don't know what your idea of Satan is, but have you realized that he is real and in your life?

Think back for a second; have you seen Satan used the techniques like the ones mentioned above in your life?

Which of these do you fall into the most? How might you prevent this in the future.

Which has been more prevalent in your life: Satan causing you to fall into sin, or God leading you into His love?

I Peter 5:8,9 Be self-controlled and alert. Your enemy the devil prowls around like a roaring lion looking for someone to devour. Resist him, standing firm in the faith, because you know that your brothers throughout the world are undergoing the same kind of sufferings.

Job 1:7 The LORD said to Satan, "Where have you come from?"
Satan answered the LORD, "From roaming through the earth and going back and forth in it."
Matthew 4:1 Then Jesus was led by the Spirit into the desert to be tempted by the devil.
Luke 10:19 I have given you authority to trample on snakes and scorpions and to overcome all the power of the enemy; nothing will harm you.
2 Corinthians 2:11 In order that Satan might not outwit us. For we are not unaware of his schemes.
Ephesians 2:1-2 As for you, you were dead in your transgressions and sins, in which you used to live when you followed the ways of this world and of the ruler of the kingdom of the air, the spirit who is now at work in those who are disobedient.
Ephesians 4:25-27 Therefore each of you must put off falsehood and speak truthfully to his neighbor, for we are all members of one body. "In your anger do not sin": Do not let the sun go down while you are still angry, and do not give the devil a foothold
James 3:15 Such "wisdom" does not come down from heaven but is earthly, unspiritual, of the devil.

The attack against Satan

The Devil went down to Georgia. He was looking for a soul to steal. He came up on a wealthy businessman named Johnny Jarret. Now, Johnny was held in high regard around town, you see. He was the president of a bank, a deacon in the church, and had the most lovely wife in town. The Devil opened up saying, "You Johnny Jarret are no good; as a person, you are worthless." You say one thing but do the opposite. The Devil went on naming Johnny's sins:

- o You stole. You stole money from innocent investors in your bank.
- o You lied. You not only lied, you lied in Church to old Mrs. Hatfield.
- o All day you think evil thoughts in your quiet air conditioned office. Thoughts of malice considered murder, disobedience to your wife considered adultery, and other ways in which you can please yourself and only yourself.

The Devil continued to fire out Johnny's past sins, as a crowd that had gathered was appalled that their Johnny would do such things.

But Johnny stood up and said, "Enough,"

"It is true, I am guilty of these sins. But I have something so much greater. God still loves me. I have committed my life to Him.

It is true as a person I am worthless, but with Jesus Christ I am worth enough to be one of God's children."

With that the Devil bowed his head, because he knew that he had been beat.

Johnny exclaimed, "Devil don't you ever come back here again, because I've told you I have Jesus Christ in my heart to take away my sins."

How does the Devil affect your life? Does he use the techniques like I mentioned in the previous chapter to get in your head? Does he put temptations in front of you that you cannot resist?

Satan may not jump up on a hickory stump and begin naming our sins. But he knows where we sin, and he knows our weaknesses. He knows where all humans struggle and where you struggle personally. He knows where to tempt all humans to where it will destroy our lives.

So how do we prevent Satan from destroying our lives? We do as the apostle Paul instructs us and put on the armor of God. Paul gives us the metaphor of a first century soldier putting on his armor and explains that we likewise should put on our armor to prepare us for spiritual warfare against Satan and evil. Paul tells us to put on a belt, a breastplate, footgear, a shield, a helmet, and carry a sword; I will attempt to explain what each mean and how we should apply it to our lives.

- **The Belt of Truth**. The belt was at the center of the body that joined all other parts of the armor. Without it, nothing stayed in place. Because we hold God as the Truth, everything in our life is bound together. Without God, nothing would be held in place; we would lack the very thread that holds it all together. It makes the praises we sing to God more than just words; it makes the words we read in the Bible more than black print, and it makes our lives have more meaning than just doing "good." The rest of our armor can function because we believe in God and believe what He can do in our lives. We must commit ourselves to believing the Word

86

as the complete truth, so that the rest of the armor will be held in place.

- **The Breastplate of Righteousness**. The breastplate obviously protected the vital organs, namely the heart. In order to clad ourselves with righteousness, we must do what is right by following God and obeying his commands. Every bit of our life should be filled with what is honorable and what is good. For by doing so, when Satan attacks us, he can only strike a quick blow that can only make us stumble, instead of striking a lethal blow to the heart.

- **Feet fitted with the gospel of peace**. Having boots/footgear protected the soldier's feet during travel, allowing for the soldier to get where he was going where he could do what he was supposed to there. The gospel motivates and protects our feet, so that we keep traveling forward in our life. Having the assurance of God's grace, we can be protected from Satan trying to slow us down or stopping us from where we are supposed to be going. We must cling to God's promises living by them each day, so that our feet will be unhindered to run towards the goal.

- **Shield of faith**. The shield protected the soldier from attacks such as swords, rocks, arrows, and spears. Our faith should be that shield that "blocks" all of Satan's attacks. Having absolute faith in God, we can block Satan's attacks from any direction. None of us have 100% faith, 100% of the time; we all let our guards down at some point during the battle. We must be constantly reminded of God's goodness and his laws so that we always put our faith in God, not giving Satan an opportunity to attack.

- **Helmet of Salvation**. Obviously, the helmet was used by the soldier to protect himself from blows to the head that would knock him out or make him become disoriented. Our hope of our salvation keeps our head in place, preventing Satan from getting inside our head making us disoriented (remember, in the last chapter how the many ways Satan does this), or even "knocked out" while we are battling sin on the battlefield.

Our salvation in God is enough to keep Satan away from our minds; therefore, allowing us to always be in full control of our body and full control of our thoughts. If we look to God and the glory of heaven, this should be enough to protect ourselves from wanting to act and think like Satan.

- **The Sword of the Spirit**. The sword was used for offensive purposes to slay the enemy and also to protect the soldier from a sword attack of another. The Word of God is our sword, and we should be using the gospel it contains to slay evil. Also, when Satan attacks us, we can use it as our defense (like Jesus did when Satan attacked him [Matt. 4]). The Word should root itself in our bodies, so that everyday we slay evil by this Spirit that is inside of us. We should proclaim the gospel letting all hear its message, penetrating their souls, killing the evil inside of them, and letting God come into this spiritually wounded body bringing it back to life. The Word should be in us; it should be in our speech; and it should be in our actions so that we may conquer evil.

- Note that there is nothing for the backside. If we turn our backs on Satan, we will have no protection from him attacking us. We should always be mindful of his presence and his strategies that he uses to attack our spiritual self.

- Also, remember that we all have different armor, different body types, and different weaknesses. A large soldier will have more body to protect and will probably have many open gaps in his armor. Some will be born with better armor than others. Some will go to the battlefield forgetting to wear a specific piece. Others will have all their armor, but they will not know how to use it. Others will gain experience using their armor and will master how to use it.

So what is your armor like?

Where are you weak, where is your Achilles heel?

What can you do to make it better?

Today, I ask that you would just take all this in - seeing how Satan attacks your life and how you can prevent it. But for the rest of the six days of this week, I ask you that you would look back and take one of the six pieces of armor and dwell on it. For example, tomorrow take the belt of truth and study in depth just about it (for the next six devotionals the message will be similar to the corresponding piece of armor, so continue reading as well). Reread what you learned from today's lesson. Think in your mind if understand the metaphor that Paul was trying to convey. See if you can come up with another practical interpretation. Examine how strong that piece of armor is on you. Think of ways in your life to how you can strengthen this armor and prevent Satan's attacks. And lastly pray about it- pray to God that he would help you put on each of these parts each day. Take 5 to 15 minutes throughout the day dwelling over these things this next week, so that you may put on the armor of God and be ready for battle.

Our spiritual lives are a constant battle of good vs. evil.
So whose side are you on?

Set out wearing the armor of God, so that you may be protected while fighting for the Lord's army.

Ephesians 6:13-18 Therefore put on the full armor of God, so that when the day of evil comes, you may be able to stand your ground, and after you have done everything, to stand. Stand firm then, with the belt of truth buckled around your waist, with the breastplate of righteousness in place, and with your feet fitted with the readiness that comes from the gospel of peace. In addition to all this, take up the shield of faith, with which you can extinguish all the flaming arrows of the evil one. Take the helmet of salvation and the sword of the Spirit, which is the word of God. And pray in the Spirit on all occasions with all kinds of prayers and requests.

Romans 16:20 The God of peace will soon crush Satan under your feet. The grace of our Lord Jesus be with you.
Ephesians 6:11 Put on the full armor of God so that you can take your stand against the devil's schemes
Colossians 1:13 For he has rescued us from the dominion of darkness and brought us into the kingdom of the Son he loves

Luke 10:19 I have given you authority to trample on snakes and scorpions and to overcome all the power of the enemy; nothing will harm you.

2 Timothy 2:3 Endure hardship with us like a good soldier of Christ Jesus

1 Peter 5:8,9 Be self-controlled and alert. Your enemy the devil prowls around like a roaring lion looking for someone to devour. Resist him, standing firm in the faith, because you know that your brothers throughout the world are undergoing the same kind of sufferings.

James 4:7 Submit yourselves, then, to God. Resist the devil, and he will flee from you.

Finding the Truth

Jeff Clemens was a wheat farmer from the small town of Pittsburgh, Iowa. Jeff had been a Christian all his life. He was one of the nicest and hardest-working men that you would ever meet. He was very active in the church, and he even thought about being a missionary before he inherited his father's farmland. But Jeff's impressive past ended on June 22, 1973, when his life was completely changed. Around 7 o'clock that evening Stacey Lane, a neighbor and close friend, came into the house to talk with Jeff's wife, Cindy. But upon walking in, she was frightened by a horrific sight. Cindy and her 7-year-old son, Jeff Jr., were on the ground dead lying in a puddle of blood. Jeff, with blood stained hands, was weeping in the chair holding his own farming tool that was covered in blood. Stacey quickly called the police, and the authorities arrived at the scene. The police handcuffed Jeff and put him in the police car; although, as they departed, he shouted all the way that he did not do it. Later, the police questioned him, and Jeff told them this story:

"I was out harvesting the wheat when at 6:30 I came in to eat supper like I do every night. But as I walked in, I saw my wife and child lying there dead on the floor. I was in shock; I pulled the wheat thrasher out of my son's chest and sat there not believing what happened. That is when Stacey Lane, our neighbor, came in and called you guys."

The authorities were very skeptic of the story to say the least. With fingerprints on the murder weapon, with the weapon being Jeff's own tool, with his bloodstained hands, and being the only person in the vicinity, the police had enough evidence to lock Jeff up. The jury of the trial was also not believers of Jeff's story. So in a quick trial, Jeff was convicted of 1ˢᵗ degree murder and was given the death sentence.

However in 1998, 25 years after the murders and Jeff's execution, a rumor came out from late drinking at a bar that a man other then Jeff Clemens killed the family. Having a slow day in the lab, the forensic scientists took out this cold case and examined the evidence. All that was left was the murder weapon. But to the scientists surprise, they found two sets of fingerprints on the tool and found epithelial skin tissue on parts of it. One of the fingerprints was, of course, Jeff's; but the other was of a man they had in database named Adam Greene. Normally, they would have just said that Adam may have just worked with Jeff and may have gotten prints on it that way. But Adam's prints were at the base of the tool, where one would grip it if they were to use it as a weapon; whereas Jeff's were on the top part as if he had just picked it out from his son's body like he said. Also, the epithelials meant that the person using it must have had a tight grip on it, indicating it was used in a struggle. The DNA on the epithelials matched Adam's DNA, which the police had in their records for several drunk driving offenses. The police brought this man in to question him.

Adam could not hold it in any longer. He confessed to the two murders, saying that as a nineteen-year-old boy he was trying to get back at his boss for working him to hard and not giving him enough money to provide for him and his wife. Adam was later convicted, and since he was willing to admit his guilt, he only received life without parole. But the nice old man, Jeff Clemens, received the death sentence. It seems that Jeff had been telling the truth all along.

The Bible calls it self the **truth,** but what is the truth? Philosophers have debated thousands of years of what is the truth. It can boggle your mind trying to find this thing called truth. For instance, we know for certain why things happen. We know when we throw a ball up in the air that it will come down because of gravity. However, we are not for sure if everything that we know is true. For if just one thing that we hold for a fact is wrong, then thousands of things we hold as true or accurate would be false. Take our example with gravity - what if one fact like the gravitational formula to find gravity is wrong. Then we would have inaccurate information about space shuttle take offs, weather balloon readings, skydiving information, airplane landings, etc. (this may not be a great example, for it seems our mathematics calculating gravity seems to be correct, but you get the point).

We have lie detector tests, but even they are sometimes inaccurate.

So how are we supposed to know the truth?

Sometimes we seem to just know the truth, especially in words from someone we really know like a spouse, child, or best friend. We can almost always tell from this person's words and expressions whether they are lying or if they truly mean it. And the same is true about the Bible; there is nothing out there that says The Bible is for 100% the absolute truth (although there is considerable more amount of evidence proving it is more fact than fiction), but we just know that it is true. As we move closer in love to God, we are able to see how the Bible is the truth. Like you can tell when that loved one is telling the truth, you likewise can see the truth in the Bible when God becomes one you love.

It is so comforting to know that when the world lets us down with all its lies and deceptions that we can turn to the Word of God knowing It is the only thing in this world that is the truth.

But when you read it, do you respond to it as though it is the complete truth?

Do you store it in your mind as being something you hold at the complete truth when it says:

"Blessed are the peacemakers, for they will be called children of God." – Matt 5:9

"Don't bow down and worship idols. I am the LORD your God, and I demand all your love." Ex. 20:5

"We know that God is always at work for the good of everyone who loves him." Rom. 8:28

"My kindness is all you need. My power is strongest when you are weak." 2 Cor. 12:9

"God raised us from death to life with Christ Jesus, and he has given us a place beside Christ in heaven." Eph 2:6

There are some things like Jeff Clemens' story that we will never know as true. For things can be disproved, discovered, or changed. Things can be true no matter how improbable they may seem. Some things we hold as true can be flat out wrong. In fact, we cannot put our trust on anything of this world as being true. That is, except the Bible - it is the infallible Word of God; it is the exact account on how we are to live.

So each time you open up its pages, are you reading it as if it is the only thing in the world that you can hold as true?

Ephesians 6:14 Stand firm then, with the belt of truth buckled around your waist

Psalm 19:9b-10 The ordinances of the LORD are sure and altogether righteous. They are more precious than gold, than much pure gold; they are sweeter than honey, than honey from the comb.

Psalm 17:2 May my vindication come from you; may your eyes see what is right

John 14:6 Jesus answered, "I am the way and the truth and the life. No one comes to the Father except through me

John 17:17 Sanctify them by the truth; your word is truth.

John 18:37,38 Jesus answered, "You are right in saying I am a king. In fact, for this reason I was born, and for this I came into the world, to testify to the truth. Everyone on the side of truth listens to me."

"What is truth?" Pilate asked

Romans 3:2-4 First of all, they have been entrusted with the very words of God. What if some did not have faith? Will their lack of faith nullify God's faithfulness? Not at all! Let God be true, and every man a liar. As it is written: "So that you may be proved right when you speak and prevail when you judge."

In Your Eyes

Maximilian Hayes was a Jewish merchant who sold clothing all across Europe to support his wife and children. In 1944, Nazi guards caught this traveling merchant and shipped him to a concentration camp, where thousands of fellow Jews and others were being held captive. Men, women, and children were all enclosed in tight quarters where they would suffer verbal abuse, torture, and even execution from the Nazi troops. Some of the prisoners had been in there for months and some for just a couple of days, but all knew what turmoil that they would go through in these type of camps. Every morning just to intimidate the prisoners from uprising, the Nazi soldiers would gather all the prisoners together in one room and demand complete silence from the congregation. The soldiers would then select 10 names at random, and have those ten executed in front of everyone. If anyone from the crowd of prisoners would stand or say a word, they too would join the other ten up on the execution platform.

On a warm, muggy summer morning, the guard had the prisoners join in the assembly, while the old chief Nazi soldier called out in a cold voice the ten names. One of the names was Maximilian Hayes. Maximilian quickly jumped up and screamed, "No, No, not me, I can't die - I have a wife and five children. I must work to keep them alive." Then to the surprise of everyone, an older man went against the strict orders, and stood up from the crowd and said, "This is

96

true. I am an elderly man. I have no wife or children. I should take this man's place." This elderly man was an ex-Catholic priest in Germany, but he had been spending the last five years of his life as a missionary to the northern part of Poland where the Nazis captured him. The chief Nazi soldier eyed the two men in a harsh stare. He eventually said, "Let it be. Let this old man be executed in the place of Maximilian Hayes." Maximilian was escorted back into the crowd, as he was in amazement of what just happened. But now Maximilian could not stand back up; he could not say another word; he could not thank this elderly man that just saved his life. For he knew that it was a blessing that they let him go once, and if given another chance, the soldiers would not think twice to ending his life. Maximilian could only look the elderly man in the eyes, and in his teary eyes Maximilian showed a sense of complete thankfulness, having a true love for this fellow man. As the bullets were shot, the old man said, "As I am dying for this man, so too did my Lord die for me."

Three more years, Maximilian would have to endure the concentration camp, to finally be one of the few to make it out alive. The first thing he did when he was released, was to find the meaning of the words that the elderly man said when he died in his place. He heard from others that the man was a Catholic priest, so Maximilian visited a nearby church hoping to find someone who had answers. Inside, Maximilian found a priest and asked him what was the meaning of the statement: "As I am dying for this man, so too did my Lord die for me"?

The priest knew right off what the intentions were before ever hearing Maximilian's story. The priest explained to Maximilian about Jesus and His love to all mankind when He died on the cross. After hours of discussion, Maximilian reached a point where he wanted to accept faith in Christ. At that moment, a tear of joy rolled from his eyes - his eyes showing the same thankfulness that they showed that day when the elderly man died for him.

Have you ever looked into the eyes of an athlete during competition, the eyes of a professor reading a book, the eyes of a couple in love while together, or the eyes of someone who just lost a close friend? Our eyes say a lot of who we are and what we do.

So what about you, when people look into your eyes, what do they see? When you are singing praises to God, do others see you giving your all? When you read God's holy word, do your eyes look like they are taking in the nourishment our minds crave? When you do an unselfish deed, do others see in your eyes that you are full of kindness? When you are in church on Sunday mornings, do your eyes show that you are happy just to be in the Lord's house?

Is your life constantly radiating the joy of being in God's love? Can people see Jesus in your eyes?

Hebrews 12:2 Let us fix our eyes on Jesus, the author and perfecter of our faith, who for the joy set before him endured the cross, scorning its shame, and sat down at the right hand of the throne of God.

Psalm 34:5 Those who look to him are radiant; their faces are never covered with shame.
Matthew 5:16 In the same way, let your light shine before men, that they may see your good deeds and praise your Father in heaven.
Matthew 13:43a Then the righteous will shine like the sun in the kingdom of their Father.
Ephesians 5:9 Live as children of light (for the fruit of the light consists in all goodness, righteousness and truth)

Discouragement

Have you ever been told by an authority figure that you can't do something, or you weren't good enough, or you don't have what it takes. It hurts deep down inside; it makes you either mad or sad; and it makes you want to quit. But sometimes that older or authority figure may just be wrong; it would not be the first time.

For example:

- In 1954, the manager at the Grand Ol' Opry fired a young man after a musical performance saying "You ain't goin' nowhere son. You ought to go back to drivin' a truck." That young man was Elvis Presley the American icon we know today.

- A prestigious Yale Professor once wrote on a paper "The concept is interesting and well-formed, but in order to earn better than a 'C', the idea must be feasible." Well Fred Smith took his idea of an overnight delivery service, which only earned him a C in college and ended up earning him millions of dollars and pioneering the delivery service industry when he found the company – FedEx.

- Mahatma Ghandi, a man that is worshipped in some cultures, said, "[The Germans] of future generations will honor Adolf Hitler as a genius, as a brave man, matchless organizer, and much more." It seems as though this wise man missed the point a little on that one.

- In 1939 the *New York Times,* the elite newspaper at the time, wrote "The problem with television is that the people must sit and keep their eyes glued to a screen: the average American family hasn't time for it." But as of today, the average American watches over 15 hours of television a week and each household owns an average of 2.5 TV sets.
- A modeling agent once told the beautiful Marilyn Monroe: "You'd better learn secretarial work or else get married."
- The founder of Digital Equipment Corporation said in 1977, "There is no reason for any individual to have a computer at their home."

And countless other insulting and demeaning remarks have been made to aspiring actors, athletes, authors, inventors, scientists, musicians, you name it. In matter of fact, most everyone who has made it famous or has had a major impact, has been told somewhere down the line "you're not good enough" "you're not smart enough," "you're too short," or "it's too hard, you'll never make it." But when we hear those things we cannot let them bring us down and make us want to quit. How do you think Elvis felt after being told that by a big shot in the music industry? I bet in bothered him at first, but I guarantee you it later motivated him to try even more. So when discouragement brings you down, make it cause you to desire your dreams just a little more and to try harder next time.

And when it comes to spiritual discouragement, I am sure Satan has mastered the art. Don't you think in our lives, that Satan is everyday telling us things such as: "everybody else does it," "it will be ok just this one time," "don't even try doing that, you can not," and "don't worry; nobody else will know." But just like in any other situation in life, we must shake off all these discouragements and live our lives like God would want us to live.

You can go through your life caving in to the criticisms of others and/or Satan, and you live your life how they want you to live it. Or you can already know what you want to do in your life, so that you will be able to accomplish your dreams.

Has discouragement from others brought you down, or has it motivated you to do greater things?

Has other's criticisms stopped you from doing something great in your life?

It's not what others think or say about you; it's what God knows and sees in you.

I Peter 3:16 But do this with gentleness and respect, keeping a clear conscience, so that those who speak maliciously against your good behavior in Christ may be ashamed of their slander.

Hebrews 12:1 Therefore, since we are surrounded by such a great cloud of witnesses, let us throw off everything that hinders and the sin that so easily entangles, and let us run with perseverance the race marked out for us.

James 1:3,4 Because you know that the testing of your faith develops perseverance. Perseverance must finish its work so that you may be mature and complete, not lacking anything.

2 Peter 2:10 This is especially true of those who follow the corrupt desire of the sinful nature and despise authority. Bold and arrogant, these men are not afraid to slander celestial beings;

Jesus Was, Is, and Will

Mary and Martha stood in shock as their beloved brother Lazarus had just died of an illness. Mary thought to herself, "Why did this have to happen?" Her close friend Jesus the miracle worker could have healed him like the many others. She thought Jesus had promised her that He would always be there for her, leaving her to question, "Was this Jesus who He said he would be?"

Roman guards stood keeping the masses of people back, while the infamous "King of the Jesus" hung on a wooden cross. The guards watched as the sky quickly became dark as night, the ground began to shake, and lightening streamed from the sky. The man on the cross let out a loud cry saying, "Father into your hands I commit my spirit." The spectators were left in awe, for no one had seen such a scene before. The guards were left asking the question, "Is this man truly who He claimed to be?"

Beth had become frustrated at a fellow co-worker named Alex at a bookstore. Beth was trying to reach out to Alex, who had made an adamant stand that Christianity was nothing more than a false hope. Countless times Beth would bring up this topic of discussion to Alex asking, "how can you deny that there is a God controlling this complex world?" Alex would never give a definite answer, but he would come back saying, "I am glad you're a Christian, but it's just not for me. I don't see it the way you do. I know it has caused you to do some great things; but for me, it would just be a burden that would only add to my already busy life." Beth questioned, "When will God ever show that He is the Supreme Being to this world?"

The answers to the three questions asked in this devotion: Jesus was, is, and will.

Jesus was there to raise Lazarus from death.

Jesus is the man He claimed to be.

And Jesus will return to this world and reign with glory.

We must always have faith in God to what He was, is, and will be.

However, our faith is not like a like a bank account in which we always have a set amount that only grows over time with interest and future deposits. But the amount of our faith varies from time to time, just like our moods. There are times when nothing can shake us from God and make us do evil, while there are others times when now that we look back on it, we wonder what we were thinking.

Our faith is temperamental. For instance look at this example: Mike, who had a fear of heights, was convinced by a group of friends to go skydiving from a airplane. Mike's friends assured him that there was nothing to worry about, and he would be glad he did it. So the group of five, took a three-hour long training course that gave them all the advice needed for them to jump out of a plane. The instructors told them that the chance of dying was almost nonexistent, that statistics showed that there was a better chance of dying from being attacked from a wild buffalo, than from skydiving. They told them that they had two parachutes in case one did not open, with each parachute able to hold up a thousand pound man. They even assured them that if for some reason they did not pull the cord to release the chute, that their electronic altimeter would automatically release the parachute for them at 5,000 feet. With all the advice and safety procedures, Mike and his friends felt more than ready to jump. However, butterflies started to flutter inside Mike's stomach when the plane began taking off. He began to get scared when he looked out the window of the plane and saw cars becoming like little ants and houses becoming like little dots. The door opened and two of Mike's friends jumped out; Mike grew terrified when he saw these men, who were in right there in the plane with him, just step out and descend at speeds at over 120 mph. It was then Mike's turn. He looked down and saw how far up he was, and he could not do it. His friends yelled at the top of their lungs, "Just Jump." For over a minute, Mike sat there with his legs trembling unable to move. Eventually one of Mike's friends pushed him out. Although scared to death, Mike was able to pull the chute open and land safely on solid ground.

Mike knew how to do it, he heard all the assuring talk on how safe it was, and at one time, he was more than ready to jump; but when Mike got up there, all this left his mind.

This is how we are like a lot of time. Sure, right now while reading this, you may have the faith to take on anything, but when you are faced in real life with the conflict, situation, or experience you may do differently. I have always wondered what I would do if a man in front of me in line at the bank, pulled out a gun and demanded money. Sure, right now in my mind, I would: try to tackle the man, wrestle away his gun, and be the hero; but if I was actually in that situation would I do the same? The same is true about our spiritual life: sure, right now in our minds we would do what is right and trust God, but in real life would we still have the same faith?

We as Christians must practice our faith. We know God was, is, and will; but do we show it and live by it. I've learned a lot about resisting sins, forgiving others, and doing right, but I have yet to gained the faith I need to do these things.

So how do we improve our faith? We can spend all day learning more about what is right, but if we do not put these things into practice, it is no good. We most gain an appreciation for these things, until we love doing them.

It is not learning God's Word, but learning to love God's Word in which faith is built.

When we love doing right, we do not have to think about it – it comes natural and we feel comfortable doing it. Like a child who has grown to love his mother but has grown to hate his abusive father, it would be unnatural for the boy to want to chose to be around his father when he has the choice of being around his loving mother. When we are given the choice to follow sin or follow what is godly, we chose the one we feel more comfortable with – the one we love. Faith boils down to love. If we truly love God, faith becomes natural to us.

Many times everyday, we have the choice to put our faith in either God or Satan – who do you chose?

Does your Faith in God and Jesus make you do miraculous things?

Do you need greater faith in your life?

What would help your faith more: learning more about God or loving God more?

You learned that God was, is, and will, but have you learned to love it?

I Peter I:8,9 Though you have not seen him, you love him; and even though you do not see him now, you believe in him and are filled with an inexpressible and glorious joy, for you are receiving the goal of your faith, the salvation of your souls

2 Peter I:5-7 For this very reason, make every effort to add to your faith goodness; and to goodness, knowledge; and to knowledge, self-control; and to self-control, perseverance; and to perseverance, godliness; and to godliness, brotherly kindness; and to brotherly kindness, love.

Mark I I:20 Have faith in God," Jesus answered. "I tell you the truth, if anyone says to this mountain, `Go, throw yourself into the sea,' and does not doubt in his heart but believes that what he says will happen, it will be done for him.

John 7:38 Whoever believes in me, as the Scripture has said, streams of living water will flow from within him

Romans 4:16 Therefore, the promise comes by faith, so that it may be by grace and may be guaranteed to all Abraham's offspring—not only to those who are of the law but also to those who are of the faith of Abraham.

Colossians 2:6,7 So then, just as you received Christ Jesus as Lord, continue to live in him, rooted and built up in him, strengthened in the faith as you were taught, and overflowing with thankfulness

I Thessalonians 4:14 We believe that Jesus died and rose again and so we believe that God will bring with Jesus those who have fallen asleep in him.

Hebrews 11:32-34 I do not have time to tell about Gideon, Barak, Samson, Jephthah, David, Samuel and the prophets, who through faith conquered kingdoms, administered justice, and gained what was promised; who shut the mouths of lions, quenched the fury of the flames, and escaped the edge of the sword; whose weakness was turned to strength; and who became powerful in battle and routed foreign armies.

I John 5:9 -11 We accept man's testimony, but God's testimony is greater because it is the testimony of God, which he has given about his Son. Anyone who believes in the Son of God has this testimony in his heart... And this is the testimony: God has given us eternal life, and this life is in his Son.

Kee's Amazing Hope

Dr. Alexander Welton was a linguistic genius who used his talents as a missionary to foreign lands. Dr. Alexander was part of the Wycliffe Missionary Group that would go to an illiterate nation, learn the language of the people, create an alphabet using their syllables, teach them how to read, and eventually get them to read scripture. The process was long and complicated, but the work of putting the Word of God in these people's hearts and the knowledge to read in their minds was worth the 5-15 years of work.

Dr. Alexander had been spending four years at a beautiful tropical island in the East Indies, and his team had almost gotten the language down and was able to communicate to some of the Indians. One Indian named Kee-wa-ta was able to understand God and would commit his life to Christ. Though the rest of the Indians were receptive of the white man's service, they would not commit their lives to this thing they did not understand called God. They viewed Kee-wa-ta as a traitor for accepting God.

One day, Dr. Alexander was badly struck by a rusted shovel from one his colleagues, as they were working to dig a ditch. The wound would get infected and turn into blood poisoning. They team had to ship Dr. Alexander out on a float plane as soon as possible to get some antibiotics or else the doctor would perish. Kee-wa-ta took them to a beach where they could signal the float plane that they had radioed for. The whole team of fifteen had to go with him Dr. Alexander on this plane heading to the Philippines because they knew if several left, that the few left behind would be weak against an attack by the natives. Kee-wa-ta, left standing on the beach, asked what he was supposed to do, because he knew if he returned that the tribe would kill him. One of the missionaries asked if he could live off the fish and coconuts on that beech, staying away from the village until they got back in a week. Kee-wa-ta did not know how long a week was, but he nodded his head. Then a missionary told him to "do that until we get back (in translation)."

Well it ended up that Dr. Alexander would tragically die on that plane ride to the hospital. The team decided that without their great leader that they would not be able to continue, for Dr. Alexander was solely responsible of the alphabet, and no one knew linguistics or the native language like him. So the team never returned to the island.

However, Kee-wa-ta was always waiting for them. After months and months of being alone, Kee-wa-ta wondered if they would ever come back. "How long was a 'week'?" he wondered. But Kee-wa-ta remembered them saying to always believe that God would be there for Him, no matter what the situation. He was reminded of a new concept called "hope" that the men taught him meaning, that as long as he believed that he would receive a peace greater than one could imagine. So he kept on believing; for years he would survive by himself off the land while reading the translated Bible consisting of the following: Psalm 23, Matthew 5-7, Luke 22-24, John 3:16, and Romans 8:28. He would go on and memorize these verses and pray to God, even though no missionary ever taught him to do these things. Finally 10 years after Dr. Alexander death, Kee-wa-ta spotted a large ship with a white man on board. He ran for miles to chase down the spot where it had dropped anchor. The boat was an expensive yacht owned by a retired millionaire named Marshall Clark, who was just enjoying life in the Pacific Ocean. Kee-wa-ta swam out to the ship while keeping one hand over the water to keep his scriptures dry. Kee-wa-ta quickly saw that this man was not Dr. Alexander, so he hesitated and stood in silence for some while, as did Marshall who was scarred out of his wits of this bearded Indian.

Finally, Kee-wa-ta tried to communicate with Marshall showing him his Bible and saying in his own tongue the verses that he memorized. Marshall was not a believer, but he recognized that on the paper that Kee-wa-ta was holding, were parts of the Bible with a foreign text written above each line. Marshall knew nothing about the Wycliffe missionaries who had visited the island a decade before, and he knew that the inhabitants of this island were savages that did not have a written language. Marshall did not know if this Indian was a prophet or if he was carrying a missing part of the Bible. Regardless, he figured that this Indian could make him some serious dough back in the states, so he locked Kee-wa-ta up in a compartment of his ship, and he had his captain to turn the ship around and head back to San Francisco, CA. Back in the states after a long investigation by historians and two journalists, the group was able to trace this man back to one of the Indians that the great Dr. Alexander witnessed to and had written about in his journal (which had been published after the doctor's death). They also found that Kee-wa-ta lived alone on a deserted beach for ten years in hope of the doctor coming back. Kee-wa-ta would live 18 years in the U.S., where he would pick up on some of the English language; although, he never really mastered it. A traveling evangelist would take him around the nation telling of this man's great story: a story of hope.

Is your hope in your life that strong? Sometimes our hope in heaven is the only thing that can make us have joy in this hopeless world. For we cannot be content with anything of this world; all will leave us with wanting more. That is, except God. For when our hope is in God, we can long for peace, happiness, self-worth, and love; and we will receive it.

It is not like God has asked us to stay on a deserted island for ten years, believing in a new concept that we do not fully know. God has written the whole Bible showing us what he can do and telling us what to do, so that we may have confidence of the glory to which is to come.

Hope is not just reading and understanding God's plan for our future, but hope is knowing and longing for that in heaven.

Your hope in your life will determine how you will live each day.

I suggest that you would constantly remind yourself throughout the day of the hope we have in Jesus and heaven. When he wake up in the morning glance at the sunlight beaming into the windows; at night, view the twinkling stars and beautiful night's sky; watch a little boy try to follow his father's advice on how to swing a baseball bat; read one of the great miracles in the Bible, or do something each day that will fill you with the hope that one day you will be in heaven. For in heaven, you will be filled with a feeling that is far greater than any other touching moment in your life.

Our hope should be across the finish line of life. Because if our hopes are in the glory of God, we can receive the celebration, which He has planned afterwards for us, while we are still running the race of life. If our eyes are on God, we can experience God, if our eyes are on this world, we can only experience the things of this world.

Many with little have more because of their hope.

Ephesians 1:18 I pray also that the eyes of your heart may be enlightened in order that you may know the hope to which he has called you, the riches of his glorious inheritance in the saints

2 Corinthians 4:18 So we fix our eyes not on what is seen, but on what is unseen. For what is seen is temporary, but what is unseen is eternal.

Psalm 65:5 You answer us with awesome deeds of righteousness, O God our Savior, the hope of all the ends of the earth and of the farthest seas,

Romans 8:23–25 Not only so, but we ourselves, who have the firstfruits of the Spirit, groan inwardly as we wait eagerly for our adoption as sons, the redemption of our bodies. For in this hope we were saved. But hope that is seen is no hope at all. Who hopes for what he already has? But if we hope for what we do not yet have, we wait for it patiently.

Colossians 1:27 To them God has chosen to make known among the Gentiles the glorious riches of this mystery, which is Christ in you, the hope of glory.

2 Thessalonians 2:16, 17 May our Lord Jesus Christ himself and God our Father, who loved us and by his grace gave us eternal encouragement and good hope, encourage your hearts and strengthen you in every good deed and word.

1 Peter 1:13 Therefore, prepare your minds for action; be self-controlled; set your hope fully on the grace to be given you when Jesus Christ is revealed.

1 John 3:3 Everyone who has this hope in him purifies himself, just as he is pure.

Powerful Words

RedEarth was the son of the Kiowah Indian Tribe leader. The tribe lived in the Midwest during the time of the early 1800's. The Kiowah Tribe was going through rough times: the White man kept taking more and more of their lands, new diseases and alcohol were plaguing its members, and other Indian tribes were fighting for their land since the White man had already taken theirs. At this moment in time, the Osage Indians, who were known to be tall and strong warriors, threaten to take away the last bit of the Kiowah lands, which had been sacred to their tribe for hundreds of years. The Kiowah Indians had little defense against this powerful tribe. The few men that were able to fight, were afraid that they would soon die to the hand of their powerful foe. RedEarth, being only a sixteen-year-old boy, was as frightened as any. RedEarth and his father rarely talked, but on this occasion RedEarth would go up to his father and explain that he was very nervous and incredibly worried. He questioned how he could fight these mighty warriors that threatened their land.

The chief would pause and look at his son for a moment. Then he got up and said (in translation), "My son, your feelings right now are of a boy; your actions of the battlefield will be of a man. You can, You will, and You will be my pride."

These words hit RedEarth with such power; he was now ready to fight.

The next day the sixteen-year old RedEarth would run to the front of the battlefield prepared to fight. There, RedEarth tied the end of a rope to his leg and the other end to a spear. He then throw the spear in the ground, so that he could not run away from his spot on the battlefield. At that spot, RedEarth would take out the family's hickory bow and slay dozens of Osage Indians that day. By noon, the Osage were able to kill this Kiowah warrior, but RedEarth's courageous actions prevented the Osage Indians from taking over their land. The Kiowahs held RedEarth as a hero, and his actions were all from being motivated by a few powerful words.

We too have powerful words spoken to us by our leader – God's Holy Word in the Bible. While many writers have written many inspirational writings, not one of them has had the power of the words of the Bible. Most Christians know this feeling too well. We read/hear a passage that touches us, and we have a feeling inside of us that makes feel like we can do anything. We want to show love to God and give him praise, and we feel like we are a better person. Many call this feeling the fire or flames that are inside of us.

This fire is so important to have within us, for when it is inside us, we can accomplish the impossible.

However, the trick is having these flames last longer than the Sunday we hear that sermon in Church, or longer than the day we read the devotional/Biblical passage. This is why we must be continually reading the Bible. (Although devotional/spiritual books like this one are helpful in our walk with God, it is by no means the Bible, and you should not just read it over the Bible.)

For the Bible is our **spiritual nourishment**, and this nourishment fuels these flames and energizes our efforts to reach where God wants us to be. When we are hungry for physical food, our bodies feel weak; we feel dizzy; and it is hard to concentrate. But when we do have that nourishing meal, our strength is revitalized, and we feel so much better. When we starve ourselves by not reading the Word, we will have the same symptoms: being weak and having a hard time concentrating over spiritual matters.

And when Satan knows that he has an easy prey, he will sure attack.

The Bible also represents itself as a **sword**. A sword that serves defensively by protecting ourselves from Satan and sin, and offensively by combating sin to influence the outside world. This is why memorizing scripture is so important. I will be the first one to admit memorizing scripture is boring, tedious, and definitely not my strong point, but it is so important to have in your life. For it allows you to:

- resist certain sins
- gives physical evidence in witnessing to others (instead of explaining to them what you believe in your own words, which believe me no matter how intelligent you are, God's Word always sounds better)
- puts yourself in a better mood
- calms yourself down in a tense situation
- allows you to instruct other Christians when they are doing wrong or to answer their questions
- and serves as a reminder to do what you have learned in your reading of the Bible.

Select a couple verses from the passages I give you at the end of each devotion. Write them down on a note card, take them with you, and look at them when you have say, 30 seconds of free time. Memorizing just one or two a week can be such a tremendous help.

The Bible also calls itself the **truth** (Remember what was said in "Finding the Truth").

Having time to discuss, study, mediate over, memorize, and most importantly, read the Word is so very important. Without reading the Bible, we are basically not eating spiritual food and this leaves our bodies weak, unable to repair themselves, and having no motivation/energy. Without reading the Bible, we are going out in the world unprotected, without anything for defense for the sins that come our way. No only that, but we also lack the power to eliminate sin from the world. Without reading the Bible, we are setting out on this voyage called life with no map or directions telling us where to go. The result is that we usually follow the direction that everybody else takes.

God gave us the Word telling us which way to go. Life is like a maze, where God created every turn and every wall, and we are the rats running inside. God already knew ahead of time how to make it through the maze, and he gave us these instructions on how to make the choices to get us to the goal.

How much time, **what** time a day, **where** you read it, and **which** part of the Bible to read are not the questions you should ask yourself today, for these things do not matter; any choice is a good choice. But the question you should ask yourself is, "**Why** am I reading the Bible?"

I encourage you to give your whole selves to reading God's word, and give your greatest efforts in trying to obey its commands. Then you will see that the Powerful Words of God motivate you to doing the unthinkable, and you will clearly find **why** reading the Bible is so important.

Hebrews 4:12 For the word of God is living and active. Sharper than any double-edged sword, it penetrates even to dividing soul and spirit, joints and marrow; it judges the thoughts and attitudes of the heart.

I Thessalonians 2:13 And we also thank God continually because, when you received the word of God, which you heard from us, you accepted it not as the word of men, but as it actually is, the word of God, which is at work in you who believe.

Psalm 85:8 I will listen to what God the LORD will say; he promises peace to his people, his saints— but let them not return to folly.

Luke 11:28 He replied, "Blessed rather are those who hear the word of God and obey it."

I Peter 2:2 Like newborn babies, crave pure spiritual milk, so that by it you may grow up in your salvation, now that you have tasted that the Lord is good.

Pray without Ceasing

Allen Dobson grew up in a small town in the state of Connecticut. Allen was a devout Christian, who loved the Lord as much as anybody. Allen's dream was to lead people to Christ. However, Allen was a timid type of guy who spoke with a low, soft voice that usually went by unnoticed. No matter how hard he tried, almost every attempt of leading some one to know God resulted in another missed opportunity. Although Allen was not blessed with an evangelic talent to spread the Gospel, he always lived a life of example in his community. In his late twenties, Allen would meet the girl of his dreams, and in a couple of years, they would get married and have two kids, Robert and James. The Christian father brought up the boys having a fear of the Lord, and he cared for his sons deeply. Each night Allen would include in his nightly prayer before bedtime that God would bless his boys, so maybe they could have that impact on the world like he desperately wanted to have in his life. Every night Allen would not forget to mention his sons in his prayers. Even though it seemed very routine, every time he said it - he meant it with all his heart.

Time went by and the oldest brother, Robert, graduated from seminary school where he would go on to preach at a Church and change the people's hearts in the same community that his dad lived in. His father, who greatly wanted that to do this in his life, was so proud of his son. The younger brother James, however, inherited his father's shyness. James knew if he followed in his brother's footsteps that it would make his father proud, but he knew he was not cut out to be a leader. However, this did not stop God from working in his life. This James became the Dr. James Dobson that we all have heard today whether it is in his radio commentaries, large seminars, or best-selling novels. Dr. James Dobson teaches on parenting to millions, and to this day he knows he had the best parent a man could have – a father that cared so much for his children that everyday of his life he prayed for them. His father never stopped praying for him. Although, he saw James facing the same troubles that he faced when reaching out to others, he prayed that God would bless his life and manifest his talents so that he could have a great impact for the kingdom of heaven. I would say that Dr. James Dobson overcame his troubles.

What are your prayers to God like?

When you truly desire something, do you pray in a manner like Allen Dobson did?

Jesus tells us to pray without ceasing for the things we desire. We most constantly go to the Lord in prayer. Asking for it once is not enough; pray over it all the time, and pray like you really want it. There is a big difference in praying a repetitive prayer and praying for the same thing that you long for. God wants us to pray to Him often.

Being sincere and praying about the same thing over and over again shows that you really want this one thing. Why would God bless you with great gift of leading others, if you were not committed to wanting to lead others? This is why we must be in constant prayer - showing to God that we will truly committed to this one thing.

Also, examine your attitude to God when you pray. When you pray to God, are you going with an attitude like you are talking to the most Holy God who is listening to everyone of your request, or are you merely saying words that sound good? Are you thinking of others and how you can impact the kingdom of God, or are you just praying for blessings for yourself? When you pray in front of people, do you pray something that sounds eloquent, or do you pray from what comes from your heart? When you pray to God, are you coming to God, or are you bringing your troubles to Him?

God loves you. He wants more than anything to bless you, His child, with the greatest gifts of heaven. We must simply come to Him wanting and asking for these gifts in our lives.

If you have a problem, if you have a desire, if you have something that you want God to do in your life – take it to the Lord in prayer.

I Thessalonians 5:17 pray continually;

Psalm 5:3 In the morning, O LORD, you hear my voice; in the morning I lay my requests before you and wait in expectation

Matthew 6:5, 7-8 And when you pray, do not be like the hypocrites, for they love to pray standing in the synagogues and on the street corners to be seen by men. I tell you the truth, they have received their reward in full.

And when you pray, do not keep on babbling like pagans, for they think they will be heard because of their many words. Do not be like them, for your Father knows what you need before you ask him.

Matthew 21:22 If you believe, you will receive whatever you ask for in prayer."

Philippians 4:6 Do not be anxious about anything, but in everything, by prayer and petition, with thanksgiving, present your requests to God

Ephesians 6:18 And pray in the Spirit on all occasions with all kinds of prayers and requests. With this in mind, be alert and always keep on praying for all the saints.

I John 5:14 This is the confidence we have in approaching God: that if we ask anything according to his will, he hears us.

Patriotic for the Lord

Sam McConnell was a retired marine that served for the U.S. military forces in the first Gulf War. In 2002, Sam was invited to the Green Center in Houston, TX for a special banquet honoring those who fought in the first conflict over in Iraq. At the banquet, a patriotic video portrayed the triumphs of the war, the memories of soldiers lost, the pains from having to endure the adverse conditions in the desert, the joys of hearing from loved ones at home, and all the many other emotions associated during war. By the movie's end, there was not a dry eye in this room filled with some of the toughest and bravest men in the world. Sam lost a brother, 12 friends in the marines, and his own left arm for the sake of this war. But when he saw that American flag rise at the end of the video, he knew that the price he paid was well worth the opportunity to live in this great country. For Sam, the love of freedom and all that comes along with it, is worth the price he paid fighting for his country.

In times like a 4th of July firework show, I have had such a strong feeling a patriotism – a feeling that was so great, that I would be willing to lay down my life for my country. During such times as these, all problems and worries seem to fade from your mind, and you are truly thankful for what you have. During such times, we seem to have a sense of unity – people that may seem different on the outside, realize that inside we are all the same. We realize that we are all are fellow citizens under this one nation. I've seen two men who greatly hated each other, turn their arguing into an embrace of forgiveness after seeing they had a common bond as common members of this same great nation.

I remember the days after 9/11 when those firefighters raised that flag above the rubble at ground zero. The inspiring scene touched all of America. We wanted to do something for our country; we were thankful for our freedom and for our lives – we were left with a patriotic zeal for our country.

And how about the times when that Olympic athlete stands atop the podium as the Star-Spangled Banner is being played. At that moment, we are proud for the athlete, our country, and our right to be called an American.

The tears falling at the mere sight of the flag, the emotions at the firework show, the feeling of the 9/11 scenes, and the triumphs of a champion on the Olympic podium are all examples of this country's patriotism – or the love for one's country.

This love over the centuries has caused men to give all they had to keep that flag of freedom flying high in the sky.

All of this has been possible because of that one thing – love.

Love of this country, not our money, natural resources, exports, or great presidents have made this country great.

And this is just the love of one's country; think of what the love of our life (that being God) should be. God's love to us is far greater than any other love of this world.

God's love - not decrees from rulers, great stories that make up the Bible, believing what our parents believe, or being afraid that we may go to hell - has caused millions of lives to be devoted to God.

Just like when war veterans see the American flag, when we Christians see the cross, we are deeply touched by this symbol that means so much to us.

Like with the firework display, when we take in the glory of God, we are struck with awe and are left with a feeling where all pain and worry go away; and we are only able to think about that unexplainable feeling that comes from walking with the Creator of the universe.

Like when we saw those firefighters raise that flag, we too feel God working within us, marking our sinful/disastrous life with a sign of His grace and love.

Like the athlete who gives his all in his competition and is rewarded by triumphing atop the podium, we too feel Jesus giving it His all on the cross, only to rise from the dead triumphing over our sins.

As many in the armed services have paid the price for our freedom, so did Jesus pay the price by dying for all our sins on the cross.

Is the love of God - the love of the most important thing in your life – more evident than these acts of patriotism?

Does your love unify you with another because you know that person is a fellow citizen in God?

When you are with God, does everything else (pain, worries, depression, and fears) leave you, and the peace that only comes from God rushes in?

Do you have such an intense feeling for God, that you know you would be willing to die for Him?

Many may have never felt this feeling of love. And for others it may be too much like the firework show – in that it only comes only once a year.

But what about today? Everyone can experience this love whether they have experienced it hundreds of times or whether they have never experienced it before. Read the Bible, pray to God, sing praises, or do anything in which you just long to be with Him; then you will not miss this feeling of joy, this feeling of complete happiness, this feeling of bliss.

Would you consider yourself being patriotic for God's kingdom?

Romans 12:11 Never be lacking in zeal, but keep your spiritual fervor, serving the Lord

Galatians 5:13 You, my brothers, were called to be free. But do not use your freedom to indulge the sinful nature; rather, serve one another in love.

Psalm 119:20 My soul is consumed with longing for your laws at all times

John 8:36 So if the Son sets you free, you will be free indeed.

Galatians 5:1 It is for freedom that Christ has set us free. Stand firm, then, and do not let yourselves be burdened again by a yoke of slavery.

1 John 4:12 No one has ever seen God; but if we love one another, God lives in us and his love is made complete in us.

Fearing the Lord

Sharafi Ali was a merchant of spices that was from Neravo, Turkey. Like most of the population from Turkey, he too was a Muslim as his last name showed his Islamic heritage.

One day a band of robbers attacked Sharafi's on the corner on the street and beat him with clubs. They proceed to steal his money and as many bottles of spice as they could carry. Sharafi was left half dead on the street. Sharafi was picked up by a man and carried to a home where the man took care of Sharafi's wounds. The man brought comfort to all of Sharafi's pains and injuries, and even the man's words seem to bring comfort to Sharafi's mind. After three days of rest, Sharafi's swelling of his eyes had gone down enough for Sharafi to open them just enough to vaguely see around him. He could not tell where he was or what exactly the man looked like, but he could see where the man was in the room. He looked toward the man and asked, "Who are you? Why are you caring for me?"

"I am a man not from this region, I have been sent by God to rescue you."

"Allah, is looking after me?"

"No, my son, the God of Israel, the God of Heaven and Earth that rules over all things visible and invisible."

Then something amazing took place. Sharafi with his eyes that could barely see, looked at the man, and the man seemed to have a mysterious aura around him as if he were shining. The words he spoke began to hit Sharafi's heart. For hours, which Sharafi later writes felt like a few minutes, the man began to proclaim the gospel of God. Sharafi's life was changed, and on that bed Sharafi accepted Jesus Christ as his Savior.

During this time, a verse from Hebrews especially stood out to Sharafi. It reads, "The Lord helps me! Why should I be afraid of what people can do to me?" The verse helped him to heal mentally from what the robbers did to him, and it helped him to set a statement that he would live his life by.

The next two days, Sharafi's body healed with remarkable speed. With the man nowhere to be found, Sharafi got up and did what he knew he had to do. He went back to his home for a week, where he fasted and did nothing but read a Bible that the man had given him. From there, he left his shop and hometown of Neravo to tell the world of the true God of this earth. From city to city, Sharafi would go throughout Muslim nations proclaiming The Gospel on the streets. He feared nothing, for he gave his life to God, and there was nothing that man could do to him that would cause him fear. His body could only be hurt, but Jesus could not be taken away from inside of him; his stomach could only grow hungry, but his heart would always be satisfied with Jesus; his life could only be ended, but a greater life would only begin. Sharafi would powerfully preach the word of God without worry or fear. Several would listen to this man's powerful words on the streets, but sooner or later Sharafi would end up being spat upon, cursed, beaten, or thrown in jail. Yet the Lord was with this man, and Sharafi always made it out of whatever situation he was in, and he was able to keep preaching to many nations.

After eleven years of preaching the gospel to thousands, Sharafi was arrested in a northern region of Pakistan. Apparently the dictator of the region had a daughter that had listened to Sharafi's message and converted to Christianity. The dictator came up to the shackled Sharafi and told him to renounce the God that he had preached to his daughter, or else torture from his men would ensue.

Sharafi told the ruler, "There is nothing from man that I fear; I fear only the one God in heaven. I will continue to proclaim the Truth for all of my days."

The ruler then had his men torture this man by whipping him, burning him, piercing him, and stoning him. But Sharafi would just take the beatings and say nothing, only letting out cries of pain. The men would torture Sharafi until he passed out from the pain, but Sharafi would never give in. The dictator offered freedom if Sharafi would only tell his daughter that Jesus was not the Savior, even if he did not mean it. But Sharafi would not agree. So the king decreed that Sharafi be killed, and his killing should be done in such a way that it humiliated both Sharafi and God. The soldiers, upon Sharafi's request, decided to hang Sharafi on a cross making him die the same slow, humiliating death of Jesus. They would set up the cross in the center of town for all to see. They were not familiar with this execution style, so they first tied him with rope onto the wooden cross. But Sharafi, having a look in his eyes that showed no fear, glared at the soldiers and said, "nail the spikes in me," as he wiggled his fingers, indicating to put them in his hands. So upon Sharafi's request, the soldiers nailed his hands and feet to the cross, but where they nailed his hands was more close to his knuckles (instead of in the center of the palm, like it was done in the Roman times) a difference that would prolong the slow execution.

They raised the cross up, and Sharafi used his high position to echo his voice across the whole city. At first the crowd made fun of him, "The follower of the false prophet is following that prophet's death." They spat upon him and cursed him. But Sharafi relentlessly voiced out the Gospel. By day two and three, people were starting to listen and the words that Sharafi was preaching was beginning to take root in them. For some, it changed their lives. By day four, all the townspeople saw how much pain that this man was in, and they saw how he kept on preaching in what he believed. Instead of making fun of him, they began to feel sorry for him; people were now weeping and wanted him to be freed. By the fifth day, the ruler's daughter tried to free Sharafi. The ruler knew that it was time for all this to end. So he stopped his daughter, and he ordered his men to set up their spears and swords in the ground in front of Sharafi's cross. The soldiers were then instructed to drop the cross and let Sharafi land upon these weapons.

As the cross was being dropped, Sharafi let out his last words yelling, "Lord I have nothing to fear, I Love You, Jesus," just before the spears pierced Sharafi's body.

Can you say that you fear the Lord? When I say this, I mean, are you in awe of his great majesty? Are willing to bow down to His name? Our lives should show this feeling, and mainly through our love to Him.

When we think of fear, we think of that feeling you get when watching a horror movie. However fear is more apparent than in the movie theaters. Fear is in our lives in all the things that we worry about. Most of us wake up each morning already worrying about what we have to do that day and if we will be able to do it. While sometimes our fears and anxiety can lead us to working hard to accomplish something good, most of the time our fears are hindrances to our lives. Our worries prevent us from enjoying life and doing what all we can possibly do. Our worries can even become greater than our faith in God. At this point, we should remember that there is nothing in this world that we should fear, for nothing can take away God and what He has done for us. So what, if you don't win that game, get that job, make that deadline, go on that one date, or have that chance again - God still loves us and nothing can take away our life in Him.

Fearing God is knowing that he is greater than anything that you may face in this world. When we set off for the day each morning, we should not be worrying about what we have to do, but we should have the assurance of what we can do. We should not be worrying if we will accomplish all that we have to do, but we should be thankful for what all we have.

God has promised that He is working for the good of those who love Him. So why is our life a battle of fear and not knowing what to expect? Our life should be like Sharafi's knowing that there is nothing to fear, except the God of the heavens.

Think for a second of a great athlete who is about to go into competition (a boxer in his corner, a quarterback lined up under center, and sprinter stepping into his blocks). Examine his face, what does his eyes look like? Do you see a face of fear? No. You think of a face of determination that is going to give it all to accomplish one thing – winning. Our attitude of life should be like that: we should have no fear, trusting only in the Lord, having the determination to do what he has called us to do - love.

Do you have a fear of things of this world?
Having the fear of the Lord will ease all other fears.

Proverbs 14:27 The fear of the LORD is a fountain of life, turning a man from the snares of death

Hebrews 13:6 So we say with confidence, "The Lord is my helper; I will not be afraid. What can man do to me?"

Deuteronomy 8:6 Observe the commands of the LORD your God, walking in his ways and revering him

Psalm 34:8 Taste and see that the LORD is good; blessed is the man who takes refuge in him.

Proverbs 9:10 The fear of the LORD is the beginning of wisdom, and knowledge of the Holy One is understanding

Mathew 6:25,27 Therefore I tell you, do not worry about your life, what you will eat or drink; or about your body, what you will wear. Is not life more important than food, and the body more important than clothes? Who of you by worrying can add a single hour to his life?

Matthew 10:28 Do not be afraid of those who kill the body but cannot kill the soul. Rather, be afraid of the One who can destroy both soul and body in hell.

Luke 12:5 But I will show you whom you should fear: Fear him who, after the killing of the body, has power to throw you into hell. Yes, I tell you, fear him

The Blessing of Setbacks

Franklin was a mediocre lawyer in the state of New York. By the time Franklin reached his thirties, he had become a little known politician. At 39 years of age, disaster struck Franklin when he was enjoying a casual swim in the ocean. Suddenly his legs went numb. His legs would never move again and his body struggled to find the energy to get out of bed – he was stricken by a classic case of the terrible disease, Polio.

Richard was that kid in class that everyone made fun of because he was slow at learning. He failed several grades, and at age 12 was diagnosed with dyslexia and other learning problems such as ADD. At age 15, he dropped out of school. Even his parents branded him as "dumb," and severely hurt his feelings by frequently telling him that he would never amount to anything.

Victoria had been very misfortunate in her life. This woman had already had seven children, but four of them died during pregnancy or childbirth, and the other three were born with being mentally retarded having serious physical problems with coordination. Only one of these three children lived past the age of four. The woman persisted to have one more child; although, doctors warned her that it too would not be a normal baby. She did end up having another baby, and it was a beautiful baby boy.

Lance at age 26 went in for a doctor's check-up after he had been couching up blood. The doctor found the cause was from testicular cancer that had spread all over his body. Doctors immediately removed several large tumors from all over his body – including two from his brain. Lance then had to go through chemotherapy everyday for the next year. The probability for living was less than 50%.

All of these figures faced extreme disabilities, weaknesses, and difficulties. And what happened to these individuals?

Franklin, the politician with polio, battled through the pain and inability to use his legs to become the Franklin Delano Roosevelt (or FDR) that we know today. He has been one of the most influential and popular presidents of this nation's history.

Richard, the "dumb" kid, who dropped out of school at 15, learned that he would never be as smart as everybody else, but he could work harder. Working over 12 hours a day, Richard Branson would rise up the business latter and eventually become a billionaire when he started his own wireless communication group, Virgin Mobile.

Victoria's son, the boy who was never given a chance by doctors, grew in five quick years to be a prodigy in music. Wolfgang Amadeus Mozart would become one of the most famous composers of music of all-time.

And Lance who had the life threatening cancer is the Lance Armstrong who has become an American hero winning a record 6-strait Tour de France tittles (a 22 day cycling challenge that is considered by some as the most grueling competition in all sports) along with being named Sportsman of the Year three times within five years.

Each of these individuals had their setbacks; they had their excuses, but none of them ever let these things stop them from reaching their dreams.

Just think of what this group of four could have done without their disabilities.

Actually, all of these individuals agree that without their disabilities that they never would have had the determination and work ethic to get them to the top. Without their disability, they would have been satisfied with just being like everyone else.

Whatever it was that Lance felt like when he was told the would never ride a bike again, whatever it was that the kids called Richard when making fun of him, and whatever it was that made FDR sit in a wheelchair for all his life - it awakened something deep down inside. It made them see that their dreams and life were flying away from them, and that they would have to run as hard as they could to reach them. It made them want their dreams even more. It was a strong sense of determination. While their disabilities made them take a few steps back, their determination allowed them to make a giant leap forward.

Upon asking Lance Armstrong how he looks forward to having to make a 3,000 mile bike ride through the mountains, in all kinds of weather, and in the midst of discouraging fans, he responded that he did it because cycling is what he loves to do; it is where his heart is.

This is the exact same approach that God wants you to have in your life with Him. When nonbelievers, who have never served as a missionary, have never given their money to the church, and have never spent their lives loving God, ask us Christians why we do it - we should respond with a smile on our face saying, "It is what I love to do, it is where my heart is."

God wants us to be determined. We all have our setbacks – some of us have certain sins that we more readily give into, some of us are not the best teachers/speakers, and some of us do not know as much scripture as others – but setbacks are only catalysts which spark our determination. And as long we are determined, we can overcome all odds and do anything.

Sin is a setback that has impaired all our lives in some way. Yet, all those that have found the Truth should be determined to reach our dreams of becoming like Christ, not giving in to our sinful desires and loving our Father with all our heart.

So what are your setbacks in your life? Have they stopped you from reaching your dreams, or has it been your own lack of determination?

For where your heart is, your life will be sure to follow.

Psalm 81:6 He says, "I removed the burden from their shoulders; their hands were set free from the basket

Romans 10:9 That if you confess with your mouth, "Jesus is Lord," and believe in your heart that God raised him from the dead, you will be saved.

I Thessalonians 2:9 Surely you remember, brothers, our toil and hardship; we worked night and day in order not to be a burden to anyone while we preached the gospel of God to you.

Taking it beyond being Inspired

Old McDonald had a farm, and on that farm was a stubborn mule. The mule was becoming a burden, for he was too old to do any work. Ol' McDonald decided that the mule's days of good use were over since he was eating more than he was worth. No one wanted to buy an old mule, so the farmer was forced into getting rid of it. He decided that he would dig up a large hole, place the mule in the hole, and bury it alive. So, the next day the old farmer and his men dug a large hole, placed the unwilling mule inside, then proceeded to fill the hole with dirt. The dirt would fall on the back of the mule; but instead of just sitting there, the mule would shake the dirt off his back to one side. The mule would keep doing this over and over until he could step up on the dirt. The men continued to shovel in the dirt, but the mule would just shake it off his back and take another step up. Before long the mule was able to take one last step out of the hole and up onto solid ground.

This was the story told by a famous politician on a whistle stop campaign tour of the United States in his bid for presidency. Harry S. Truman was able to persuade people that this mule was the U.S. who would successfully shake off the dirt from WWII and step back unto solid ground. The story obviously moved the voters into swaying their votes, for Truman won in a very tight election over the thought-to-be favorite, Thomas E. Dewey. However, the words in Truman's speeches faded away like the dust in the wind, and everyone seemed to forget how Truman had promised to relieve all the "dirt" or problems caused by WWII. Today, many other politicians tell all these inspiring stories to get the support of potential voters, yet these stories never mean anything except to bring short inspiration to its listeners.

However there has been this one man whose stories would have an effect on people for the rest of their lives. Jesus' parables and teachings have had more of an effect on this world than any other event. Although he never told a story outside a 200-mile radius of his home; he never wrote down one of these stories; and only spent three years of his life telling His message – they have forever changed the world. These stories make up part of the best-selling book of all-time, these stories are memorized in the minds of his followers, and these stories have changed the hearts and lives of all His listeners.

So are Jesus' words having an impact on you, or are they merely a politician's speech?

Has these devotions had a great affect on you?

For people to make the most out of what we have learned, we have to do more than just be inspired. I am sure you have been inspired to do dome kind of good by reading the Bible, reading a devotional like this one, or hearing a moving sermon; but have you taken this advice beyond that? - Have you used it in your life? - Have you made it a part of you?

For inspiration to fully get it into you life, one must dwell on the Word. Write down your reflections, go back and review your previous days readings, and pray to God about it as soon as finish reading it.

And specifically for my devotions, answer the questions I ask (in your head or paper). Be constantly reminding yourself of what you have learned. Process in your mind how the scriptures at the end relate to the message. Memorize one or two of these scripture. And pray to God to let you learn the things He wanted you to learn and not something in my teachings that may be flawed (for as a writer, I am only human. While I have tried my best to take everything from the Bible and have prayed continually that the Holy Spirit be with me to use me as a tool to write for God; by no means, do I want you to consider everything in here as if it were the infallible Word of God).

If you want to have more of God in your life, you must do more than just be inspired. It will take a little effort from your part. I mostly encourage prayer and writing things down. By writing things down, you reinforce in your mind what you have just learned, and you make yourself think about it in a way that makes sense to you. You don't have to purchase a fancy journal or book especially made to go along with this one, just a piece of notebook paper will do. Write the title of the devotional, the date, or topic and underneath it: reflect on what it meant to you, include some of the answers to questions I asked, apply it to your life, and write how you can do this or change something in your life.

Take time right now to skim back on the previous chapters that you have read remembering what you have learned so far. Every so often reread the chapters (skipping the story if needed) that you have enjoyed the most or the ones that you need to work at the most.

In writing these devotions, I have tried to leave you, the readers, with a better sense of God's love, and how as Christians we are to love.

Have you done anything with that which you have learned thus far?

I Timothy 4:15-16 Be diligent in these matters; give yourself wholly to them, so that everyone may see your progress. Watch your life and doctrine closely. Persevere in them, because if you do, you will save both yourself and your hearers

Joshua 1:8 Do not let this Book of the Law depart from your mouth; meditate on it day and night, so that you may be careful to do, everything written in it. Then you will be prosperous and successful.

Psalm 119:27 Let me understand the teaching of your precepts; then I will meditate on your wonders

Proverbs 4:13 Hold on to instruction, do not let it go; guard it well, for it is your life.

Isaiah 51:7a Hear me, you who know what is right, you people who have my law in your hearts:

Luke 21:33 Heaven and earth will pass away, but my words will never pass away.

John 15:7 If you remain in me and my words remain in you, ask whatever you wish, and it will be given you.

Philippians 4:8,9 Finally, brothers, whatever is true, whatever is noble, whatever is right, whatever is pure, whatever is lovely, whatever is admirable—if anything is excellent or praiseworthy—think about such things. Whatever you have learned or received or heard from me, or seen in me—put it into practice. And the God of peace will be with you.

For the Love of Money and Sex

Scott Hamsley was a 28-year-old businessman from Hilton Head, South Carolina. One day, luck seemed to come Scott's way, when he was promoted up to a high paying job at the top of the distributing company that he worked for. Scott then took his raise from his larger paycheck, and put it into stocks and real estate investments. Within the year his stock investments tripled, and a construction company building condominiums was seeking after his land that he owned. This young businessman would receive all the money he would ever need within that year. He and his wife, then bought the house of their dreams – a new three story place located on High-life Ln. located on the beach. While Scott noticed that his house was the nicest in the neighborhood, his other possessions were not. So he went out to buy a six-dollar figure car for him and his wife, a nice watch for himself, and a diamond ring for his wife that he could not afford for her when they got married. Scott's luck seemed to only increase. He was promoted to Vice-President of the distributing company that he worked for. As the money in Scott's paycheck increased, so did his spending. He bought a yacht and a motor home because he loved to travel. Scott figured that he was young, so he ought to do and see everything in the country while he still could. Scott ended up not putting in many workdays at the office to his coworker's displeasure. After a couple of months of "enjoying life," the company grew tired of Scott's hedonistic attitude and lack of work, so they voiced their opinion and had their vice-president fired. The company did not even offer him back the job where he started at in the company. The stocks that had been so strong for Scott, plummeted after 9/11. He now found himself not being able to pay his bills, and he had to sell his possessions one by one. Eventually he could not sell any more, so he then had to declare bankruptcy. Scott could not find a job and hated the life that he was living. On December 28, 2001 on his 30th birthday Scott Hamsley committed suicide.

As you can see, Money and sex (in the next lesson) are the two of the most powerful things in our culture. Look at television's most watched television show *CSI,* 90% of the motives for the murders/ crimes are from money and sex. These are two areas that everybody is familiar with, and these two things are great things when used as they are supposed to. But in America today, these are the top two things that lead to sin, and these sins are the ones that ruin people's lives.

Money is what everyone loves, it is what everyone strives for, and it is the common bond that keeps this country together. Money is everywhere and the talk of everybody: look at the millions of books that have been written singly on the sole issue of money. Whether it be how to make it, how to spend it, fiction tales of wanting/ having it, how we should keep (invest) it, and even how Christians should look at it.

Money, also, shapes our lenses for the outside world. Nowadays, we determine so many things in terms of money. For example, we determine a person's success by how much money he has in his bank account; we determine how good a president is by how the economy is doing; we look at how much a job pays before we even consider taking it; and we look at the world with money being our obsession.

But why is money a bad thing?

Money is one of those things where one never gets enough. When a reporter asked a billionaire business tycoon how much money was enough he responded, "one dollar more." Each and everyone one of us will usually have this attitude – we always want more. Think to yourself what would be the least amount of money that you could have to be perfectly content. $25,000? $100,000? a million? No matter how much you responded by the time you went spending that money, you would eventually want more.

"Money can not buy happiness." Even though is has been said a million times, it could not be more true. Sure it may give someone some happiness at first, but soon the huge house is not good enough, then the cars do not no longer provide the happiness, then the jewelry, then the yachts. Like in Scott's case we are never perfectly happy and always want more. Men who have a lot of money and buy these luxurious things admit they never really enjoy the things they have, because they already want something else before the buy and enjoy that one thing they want. For example, one that is about to buy a nice beach house by the ocean never really appreciates what he has in the house because he is already wanting and plotting how he will be able to buy a boat, so he could ride it on the ocean when he visits this beach house.

However, what makes money so powerful is not its insatiable need for more, but it is the greed that is shown to get it. What people do for money is unbelievable. People these days lie, cheat, steal, and even murder to get money. On the big screen nowadays, almost every "bad" guy is after one thing – and that is money. Things such as: all the frequent robberies from businesses/homes, credit card identity theft, the lottery, casinos, and counterfeiting show that everyone wants money and will go to any means to get it (I bet Satan just loves this). One doesn't have to go far to see this– if it has never happen personally in your life, just turn on the television any night to see some of those outrageous Court TV shows featuring those eccentric judges disputing cases about money. When we think of our dream lives, even us Christians think of having the mansions, cars, and luxuries, instead of being in heaven.

So how are we as Christians supposed to deal with money? We can by no means avoid it, for it is a must to function socially in our country. Rather, I think God wants us to live our lives being content with what we have. We cannot just let ourselves be consumed over it (if you have trouble to willingly tithe to the church or some Christian service, money is obviously an issue in your life). If we do have a lot of money – great, then you should not have to worry about finding money to provide for yourself/family to get by in life. If you don't have much – fine, then you can enjoy all the many other things in life (Also remember what Jesus said about the wealthy entering heaven; Mark 10:25). Regardless, we should be thankful for what we have. If one has a good amount of money, pray to God that your thoughts about money will not consume you and pray that you would use your money in a way that pleases God. If the opposite is your concern, ask for God to help you through your financial situation, and when help is given, you should praise God and seek ways in which you can use the money for the Lord.

How important is money to you in your life?
Is it constantly in your thoughts?
Have issues over money caused troubles in your life?
Would you rather have all the money in the world, or heaven?

I believe the old adages sum it up: you can never get enough money (that is in a greedy sense in which you are never content), money does not bring happiness, and money is the root of all evil. For Christians it must be just one of those things in our lives, not our lives after that one thing. As you live your life, be mindful of money's power and how it affects your life.

The piece of paper does not make you sin; it's how ones spends it, the thoughts about it, the obsessions over getting it, and the actions that it causes.

Ecclesiastes 5:10 Whoever loves money never has money enough; whoever loves wealth is never satisfied with his income. This too is meaningless.

Matthew 6:21,24 For where your treasure is, there your heart will be also."No one can serve two masters. Either he will hate the one and love the other, or he will be devoted to the one and despise the other.You cannot serve both God and Money.

Mark 10:25 It is easier for a camel to go through the eye of a needle than for a rich man to enter the kingdom of God."

I Timothy 6:10 For the love of money is a root of all kinds of evil. Some people, eager for money, have wandered from the faith and pierced themselves with many griefs.

2 Timothy 3:2 People will be lovers of themselves, lovers of money, boastful, proud, abusive, disobedient to their parents, ungrateful, unholy,

Hebrews 13:5a Keep your lives free from the love of money and be content with what you have,

I Peter 5:2 Be shepherds of God's flock that is under your care, serving as overseers—not because you must, but because you are willing, as God wants you to be; not greedy for money, but eager to serve;

For the Love of Sex and Money
(Part 2 of 2)

Rondell Williams was one of Scott's neighbors that lived on High-life Ln. Rondell had been happily married to his wife for three years, and for three years the two were very happy together. But one day, Rondell had a confrontation with a secretary at work and one thing lead to another, and Rondell would commit adultery. The relationship remained secret for several months until everyone at the office knew what was going on. Rondell's boss, not knowing how to deal with the situation, decided to fire the secretary and keep one of his top employees in Rondell. Rondell felt so at fault to what had happened; and not knowing what else to do, he went to a bar to drink away his troubles at a bar. At the bar, Rondell met a woman named Vanessa. He was attracted to her at first sight. After hours of talking, Rondell felt like he had known this woman for years and even called her his soul mate. The next two weeks, Rondell would leave town, telling his wife that he was going on a very important business trip, but he would actually be going to visit Vanessa in her hometown in Atlanta, GA. For two weeks everything went great until Rondell mentioned to Vanessa that he was married. Rondell promised he would sort things out, and there was no need to be mad or upset. Rondell returned home to Hilton Head trying to sort out his life. But four days later, Rondell was found dead washed up on the beach with 3 gunshot wounds in the chest. To this day, Rondell's murderer is still unknown.

Along with money, sex is one of the things that leads to most noticeable sins in today's culture; and just like money there is nothing wrong with it in itself, but almost every everyone uses it in the wrong manner.

It does not take a genius to figure out that sex is everywhere in this country. Sex is in all the latest hit songs, shown everywhere by the media, and it is in our minds. Music stars act like it is nothing to show scantly clad parts of their body, TV sitcoms cast the image of un-marital sex as part of everyday life, and pornography sweeps all across the internet.

Sexual sins are like many other common sins, in that a little action or activity will quickly snowball into greater things. You start off by just thinking of the idea. Then, you may try that one particular sin. Next, you keep doing the sin as it keeps getting deeper and deeper rooted inside you. Until finally that sin is attached in you. By this point, you are consumed by the sin. For example, think of a teenage relationship between a boy and girl. They may have a relationship that involves talking and maybe an occasional kiss, which is perfectly fine. But soon, they seem to talk about subjects like sex. Soon, they start to get more physical with their relationship, then these physical acts grow closer and closer to sexual sin, and eventually, sexual intercourse will be the next step.

Sexual sins are like a big boulder rolling down a hill –they start out rolling slowly, then just after a short distance the boulder cannot be stop, the boulder keeps picking up more and more speed, until finally it is out-of-control and there is no telling what it may destroy.

No one has control of what sexual sin is going to destroy in their life – it could give one a sexual disease, cause an unwanted child, cause one's thoughts to be centered on sexual things, and cause bad relationship with another (for various of reasons). Ask someone who has had un-marital sex (although I don't encourage you to go up to people and ask if they had un-marital sex, just someone close that you have a feeling has) and ask if the relationship between these two individuals were the same afterwards. Sex is a powerful thing, and it will change things.

Sexual sins are different than other sins because they are natural – meaning they are not learned and our bodies strive to have sex. Just remember - while sometimes it seems hard to stop ourselves to commit the sin, it is even harder to stop the boulder when it is set into motion. As money's driving force that leads to sin is greed, sex's driving force that leads to sin is lust. While I need not to go into detail over this issue, because I know countless number of preachers give this sermon on Sunday mornings, I will say that lust is something that seems so right before or in the middle of the act of sinning, but afterward it is one of those things where one knows that it is wrong. Lust and unmarital sex is an obvious sin and everyone knows that this is not just an ordinary human feeling. This is why so many Christians look at the idea of Jesus having lustful relations with any woman as being ridiculous – because they know it is wrong, and we know that Jesus would not do such a thing.

Just like money, there is not one cure-all action that prevents sexual sin in ones life. Some suffer from it more than others, but still all of us suffer from it in one shape or fashion. Most of us Christians have heard the sermons and advice to stay away from sexual sins, and it seems as though we can keep this attitude for a short period of time. But really I do not think these lessons are too much of a help. Why? Like I have already pointed out sexual sins are natural, so these temptations will always be coming back to us. However why the battle is so tough, is because we listen to a 30-minutes sermon over the wrongs of sexual sins, but by just watching a 2-hour movie we may have viewed 30 minutes of influence that is the exact opposite of that taught in the sermon at church. You can imagine by just the amount of TV/movies we watch, magazines we read, and talk we hear of how much we are exposed mentality to that which is

144

opposite taught in the Bible. For the amount we are influenced that tells us sexual sins is wrong, we hear 4 times the opposite. Just by living our daily lives we are constantly being influenced by a wave of ideas contrary to what is the Truth. This is why we cannot be taught not to have sexual sin in our life.

We must continually realize it is there and be praying about it. You must make up your mind to be pure and know that there is no other option. Praying that you stay away from certain situations and already having your mind made up, is the best you way for you to prevent any sexual sins.

Remember, like in Rondell's life, no comfort is ever found in sexual sin. And no matter how fun it may seem, sexual sin never leads to anything good.

When you are engaging in sexual sin you are walking on thin ice; so don't even try it, because if the ice breaks you are trapped and cannot get out.

Examine your life right now – do you consider your body as pure – not being marred by sexual sins?

Is there anything that is in you (that you may not even realize) that is leading you to sexual sin?

Sexual sin is something that is uncomfortable to talk about. It is something that repels unbelievers for coming to Christianity. It is something that ruins the lives of many. It is something that is everywhere in the culture. Is it something in you?

Romans 13:13 Let us behave decently, as in the daytime, not in orgies and drunkenness, not in sexual immorality and debauchery, not in dissension and jealousy. Rather, clothe yourselves with the Lord Jesus Christ, and do not think about how to gratify the desires of the sinful nature

1 Corinthians 6:13 Food for the stomach and the stomach for food"—but God will destroy them both. The body is not meant for sexual immorality, but for the Lord, and the Lord for the body

Ephesians 5:3 But among you there must not be even a hint of sexual immorality, or of any kind of impurity, or of greed, because these are improper for God's holy people.

Revelation 14:4 These are those who did not defile themselves with women, for they kept themselves pure. They follow the Lamb wherever he goes. They were purchased from among men and offered as firstfruits to God and the Lamb

We cannot always Win

Rico Thompson was a Little League baseball player from Dansville, New Jersey. Rico's life was baseball. He played in three separate leagues: one in the spring, one in the fall, and one in the summer. In the winter after his chores, Rico would practice until the sun went down. Rico would spend all of his birthday and allowance money on baseball gloves, bats, and other equipment. On all his teams, Rico was used to being the star pitcher and shortstop, and he was also known for being the best hitter in the league. Being the best, Rico always expected his team to win; in his hundreds of games Rico played, he would only lose three before middle school.

When Rico was twelve years old, he and 14 other talented ballplayers from Dansville were selected to be on a traveling all-star team that would compete against other all-star teams from different cities. Under Rico's leadership, this Danville's team easily won three straight tournaments and were crowned state champs. The team was then sent to New York City where they would play the state champions from all over the Northeast. At this regional tournament, several teams played them close, but the Dansville kids remained unbeaten and would win yet another tournament. This tournament win allowed the team to advance to the renowned Little League World Series in Williamsport, Pennsylvania.

Rico was so excited – there was going to be TV cameras, professional announcers, world-class facilities, and a chance to be called World Champs – this was what Rico lived for. Before the tournament, Rico knew that they would win, and he dreamed of hitting the winning homerun or striking out the last batter to seal of the victory.

However in the tournament, things did not go as Rico dreamed. Dansville quickly found out that the teams they were playing were also undefeated, and they also had their own superstars like Rico. Dansville was beaten first round in this double-elimination tournament by a great team from California, but the team was able to bounce and win their second game to keep their hopes alive. The third game would have to be played against a tough team from Texas, but a win would allow Dansville to get back in the winner's bracket and possibly set up a second match up against the California team in the championships. This third game was a close game that kept going back and forth between two very good teams. In the last inning, Dansville had a chance to win with Rico batting, bases loaded, down by two with two outs. However, Rico would chase after a curveball in the dirt for strike three and the Dansville's team would lose the well-fought game, ending their great season. Rico fell to his knees in tears. He did not win the game for his team; he did not get to hold up the championship trophy, and he did not do what he dreamed. Though in heartbreaking fashion, Rico did learn a valuable lesson in life: You cannot always win.

So many people live their life as if they were trying to win something. We frantically live our lives as if it is a race or contest to see who gets the most money, who holds the most power, who is more popular, who has done more, etc. But when we live our lives this way we find that we can never win. Like in Rico's case, we will eventually come across someone better or just as good. Or, we find that whatever that one thing is that we have depended on to get us through life, is the very thing that will let us down.

This is true because we were not created to be the best, to have everything, or to get everyone's attention. We were created to love God, and be a part of his kingdom.

In our lives we cannot win by gaining things of the world; we win by losing. We lose our old self whose interest is of this world, to gain a new self that seeks that which is not seen or comprehended by the world. Or to sum it up, God is the only thing that can make us complete, and this it the only means to which we ever win in life.

Most Christians feel, "yes, that I do have Jesus in my heart," and say, "I have everything I need through Christ." But most Christians still try everyday to be the smartest, richest, or even best Christian. We must look beyond this and do things for the shear love of doing it and for the love of others.

I personally, like Rico, grew up being very competitive in sports and school, and it is just natural for me to want to be the best in everything I do. But nowhere in the Bible does it tell us to be the greatest or best – only to do whatever we do out of love so that it may please God and man.

For God does not care as much if you win the Little League World Series, as much as he cares that you spent every game doing what would glorify him.

He does not care how much salary your job makes; he cares how you use your job and the money from you job to honor Him.

He does not care how big your house is; He cares if you would be willing to give up your house in order to move into His.

He does not care where you grew up, but how you are growing as a Christian now.

He does not care if you are the best, champion, greatest, strongest, or favorite of something; he just wants your love.

So do not try to succeed, win, or get ahead in life by reaching for money, fame, or power. Reach first for knowing and loving God, then live your life where God takes you.

You cannot keep trying to win in life. You must surrender (lose) your life to gain (win) it.

Matthew 10:39 Whoever finds his life will lose it, and whoever loses his life for my sake will find it.

Matthew 16:24,25 Then Jesus said to his disciples, "If anyone would come after me, he must deny himself and take up his cross and follow me. For whoever wants to save his life^H will lose it, but whoever loses his life for me will find it.

John 12:25 The man who loves his life will lose it, while the man who hates his life in this world will keep it for eternal life.

Ephesians 4:24 and to put on the new self, created to be like God in true righteousness and holiness.

Do Everything As Jesus Would Do

Walter May was a junior studying theology at the University
of Miami. Walter very much enjoyed the college and was active in
various organizations on campus. On Wednesday nights he would
always attend a guys Bible study put on by a Christian group on the
campus. On his first visit there his junior year, the speaker warned
the guys about the temptations that they would face in the upcoming
school year. The speaker said, "Guys, I got to tell you that there is
so much out there to lead you astray. You are out on your own for
the first times in your life, and you will not have parents or anyone
else there telling you what to do. And not only are you guys in a
period where many lose their faith to chase after the sins of the
world, but also you are in a city known worldwide for its party-life
and pleasure-seeking activities. So, I would encourage you not to try
to avoid the temptations, because this is impossible. I recommend
that you have someone there with you to help you out and keep you
accountable. I, personally, have a friend that writes me every week
in an email asking things like: 'have you been loyal to your wife?'
'have you given time to serve Christ?' and 'are you trying your best
to lead students to saving faith?' I will then answer these questions
truthfully, and send him similar type questions for him to answer."

After the Bible study was over, Walter noticed a new face that
he did not recognize. He introduced himself to this guy, and found
out that his name was Jared Cross who was also a junior, but he had

just transferred from the University of Texas to come to Miami that year.

"Yeah, Jared the speaker tonight was right – there's so much here to distract you in your walk with God – with all the good-lookin' girls, Frat parties, and all that goes on the strip and clubs – it is hard trying to live a godly life - it's probably a little different than what you have seen at Texas."

"Yeah, your probably right. And having an accountability partner like he said would probably not be a bad idea. I will give you my cell phone number and all, and maybe we can keep each other accountable over this next year, if you would like?"

Walter agreed that this would be a good idea, so that night they promised that they would always help each other out making sure that each other was doing what would please God.

Over the few months, the two would become great friends and would stick to holding each other accountable. It almost became like a game on how they would remind each other to do what is right. They would email each other, leave messages on the other's answer machine, and leave post-it notes in random places around each other's apartment. Occasionally they would call each other in the middle of the night or even interrupt in the middle of a class to remind each other. They asked each other questions and told words of encouragement such as the following: "Have you had your quiet time lately?" "Are you doing what is right?" "Jesus still loves you even though you made a D in Biology." "Are you thanking God for his love he has shown to you?" And Jared would always end his note, phone call, etc. by saying, "Do everything as Jesus would do." - This would become the motto for the two's friendship.

One day as Walter was walking to the grocery store, he saw a man in a business suit take out a gun and shoot a guy in broad daylight. The event happened right in front of Walter's eyes, he stood stunned not knowing what to do. He then saw the man turn and run in the opposite direction. Walter yelled, "Someone stop that man." But his shouts were in vain, for no one did anything. So Walter took off and tried to follow this man, but he tried to keep a good distance because he knew this man had a loaded pistol. Walter followed him until he ran alongside a park on the campus. There, Walter yelled once more at the top of his lungs, "someone stop this man!" Luck happened that a large Hurricane football player was in the vicinity, and he brought this man down, where a crowd helped wrestle away the man's gun from his hands. Walter called the police and told them what happened. The police officer thanked everyone there for their help, and asked Walter to come into the station to testify as a witness to the shooting. Walter explained to them the whole story, and the police thanked Walter for his courage and let him go. Upon stepping out of the police station, Walter heard a voice that said, "Stop right there, son." Walter turned around and saw four men wearing sunglasses come out of a black town car. "You're the gentlemen who witnessed the shooting on Poplar Street earlier today, are you not?"

Walter just nodded his head in silence. Then one of the men in the back took out a large briefcase and opened it. Inside was stacks and stacks of hundred dollar bills. Walter had never seen that much money in his life.

Then the man spoke up and said, "All of this money here, one million dollars, is yours, if you go back in there tomorrow and say that the guilt got to you and that the man you accused was not the shooter. And you simply blame someone else from there."

With that the men, quickly got back into their car and sped off.

Walter did not know what to do. Could he possibly tell a lie of this magnitude? "But it was for a million dollars," he thought. He could not even imagine what he could do with that money. He thought, "I'm sure I could find someone who is worthy to take the punishment for this killing; it just will not be the guy who did it, but there has to be someone in the city that deserves punishment for something." Walter did not know what to do, so he went to talk with his best friend Jared.

He told him the story of what happened to him on Poplar Street and what happened to him with the mob guys offering him the money. "Jared what do I do, I know I should tell the truth, but it is a million dollars – I would be set for life."

"I see your point, man. It is a hard decision, but it is your decision. I am not going to tell you what choice to make. But I am only going to give you the same advice that I have told these last few weeks, and that is to "do everything as Jesus would do."

Walter was torn; he did not know what to do. That night he could not sleep. It was as if one conscience was telling him, "Take the money" but the other was repeating Jared's words, "Do everything as Jesus would do."

Walter woke up the next morning and headed straight to the police station. There he sat down and talked with the detective, and said,

"That man I told you that shot the guy on Popular Street yesterday"

"Yes, Mr. Allenby"

"Yeah, him." He then let out a long sigh and said, "He was responsible for the shooting. I am 100% sure."

Walter left the police station running as fast as he could back to his apartment looking over his shoulder for any black towns car. He was anxious to tell Jared of the decision that he had made. When he got back safely to his apartment, he picked up his cell phone to call Jared, but he only got a message from the operator saying that the number was no longer a working number. He considered this strange, but laughed to himself saying, "Jared must not have paid his bills on time."

He then went over to Jared's apartment. He knocked and walked right in, but Jared was not there, nor was all his stuff – the room was completely empty. He then knocked on the door across the hall wanting to know what may have happened to his friend. But the girl he asked just looked at him strange and said, "Room 204? there has not been anyone living there this entire semester." The puzzled and worried Walter then went to check if Jared was at any of his classes, but there was no sign of him. He then went to the administration office to check if they knew something. But they found no Jared Cross in their records, and there was not even a transfer from the University of Texas that enrolled at the university last semester.

Walter got back to his apartment and found a note lying on his table. It read,

"Walter I am proud of the decision you made. You made the choice to do what is right, and the choice that would please God – that was our promise to each other from the beginning. Continue to always, 'do everything as Jesus would do.'

Jared Cross"

It was then that Walter realized that he may have had someone from heaven by him the whole time.

If you were in Walter's situation, what would you have done? If those guys with the sunglasses flashed a briefcase of 10,000 hundred-dollar bills if front of you, could you say no?

There will be times in your life when doing right is not going to come easy. Saying "no," "I'm sorry," or "I do not want to do that" will be a lot harder than you think. This is why we need someone or somebody to keep us accountable. I suggest you find someone and do, like Walter and Jared, did to keep each other doing right and making sure you are loving the Lord in your life. Find other ways to keep yourself accountable and "doing everything as Jesus would do." Hang scriptures around your house, wear a WWJD bracelet around your wrist, carry a small New Testament Bible in your back pocket, write reminders/encouragements on your hand, wear a cross around your neck, or come up with your own creative way.

Are all your actions a testament of love to God?

Would your life be any different if Jesus were holding you accountable each day?

We cannot avoid all temptations, and we cannot resist all the temptations that come our way. But we can try our best to do everything as Jesus would do.

Ephesians 5:1,2 Be imitators of God, therefore, as dearly loved children and live a life of love, just as Christ loved us and gave himself up for us as a fragrant offering and sacrifice to God

Joshua 1:9 Have I not commanded you? Be strong and courageous. Do not be terrified; do not be discouraged, for the LORD your God will be with you wherever you go.

Ecclesiastes 4:12 Though one may be overpowered, two can defend themselves. A cord of three strands is not quickly broken.

2 Corinthians 4:8 - 10 We are hard pressed on every side, but not crushed; perplexed, but not in despair; persecuted, but not abandoned; struck down, but not destroyed. We always carry around in our body the death of Jesus, so that the life of Jesus may also be revealed in our body.

Life's Choices

Benjamin Thomas was at an out-of-town convention in Las Vegas, Nevada. One night as he was riding the elevator up to his room, the elevator stopped on the second floor and a beautiful, young girl joined him there. The girl seemed very interested in Benjamin and why he was in Las Vegas. The elevator dinged and it was time for Benjamin to get off on his floor, but the woman began to follow him. "Well it was nice meeting you, – I'm sorry I did not catch your name."

"It's Veronica. And we don't have to say good-bye here, I do not have anywhere else to go tonight. I could join you in your room for a while."

Benjamin did not know where this was going, but he knew that he was going to have to make the decision of what was going to happen next. He had a wife and children at home. On the other hand, his wife would never find out, and no harm would come if say something did happen between him and Veronica that night. He was left with a choice.

Philosophers have said that the meaning of the word *life* is: a world full of choices.

And if you asked that same philosopher the meaning of the word success, he would tell you it is: a life of making the right choices.

How many choices do you think we make during a day. According to one study during a 24 hour period, a human being can make up to one billion conscious choices. Just think right now you have the choice of whether or not to read this devotional; you have the choice to sit upright, slouched, cross-legged, standing up, with a pen in your hand, or a finger twirling your hair. Some of our choices are easy to make, like putting on clothes. On some choices there are many options to choose from, like picking out which clothes in our closet to wear. Other choices have two good situations, like choosing between a vacation to the beach or a vacation to the mountains. But most of the choices we make are right, or they are wrong. We can get a math problem right or not. We can either dial the right phone number or not; we could pick the right numbers for the lottery or not. But the only choice that matters is - if you chose to love God or not.

With the uncountable number of choices we have in a lifetime, only one matters. And that is to accept God. We can make all the right choices, but only one lets you live life fully. It's simple, you have the choice to believe in God. Then, you have the choice of whether or not to love him, and scripture says that accepting Jesus into your heart is enough for anyone to inherit a life ten times greater than a life of making all the best choices here on earth. Scriptures also says that our love for God should motivate us to make the right choices, becoming more like Christ each day.

So ask yourself, is one of your main desires trying to make the right choices each day? What about the next week - will you make the choices that you know are right? What about down the road, are you confident that the choices you make are worth being called a Child of God? True, it is impossible to make all the right choices all the time, but it is much easier for you to make the choice before you are given the actual choice. For example a Christian should know the answer or response to a choice like unmarital sex, shoplifting, cheating for a friend, Internet pop-ups, taking drugs, and adultery while on a business trip to Vegas. Sure everyone will be tempted by these things, but the one that will make the right decision is the one that already knows his decision before the sin is before him.

Most of the time the right choice requires: more than a simple *yes* or *no,* or more effort, or more trouble, or hurting someone feelings, or maybe even causing others to look at you in a negative way. But for me personally I would rather look "uncool" or give a little extra effort, than to have to account for my sin in front of God after I die. Sometimes the situation will have so many other factors, like for example: "everybody else does," or "no one will ever know." But still that one choice you make will be right or wrong – and it is only up to one person (that being yourself) to make the decision.

Going back to Benjamin Thomas' example. He was right; more than likely, no one would ever know, and no harm may have resulted if he sinned that night. We are saved by God's grace, so as long as Benjamin goes back to God with a truly broken heart, he could be forgiven. So nothing bad would come from that sin, right? Wrong.

For every choice we make, we make a choice that turns us one way. God is one direction and Satan in the other. If Benjamin were to give in to his sinful desires that night, he would turn towards Satan. Then though he may not be realizing it, he would still be walking in that direction in his life. Other temptations will come his way and it will be nothing for him to keep going in the direction that he is already heading; turning back is more difficult. As one is walking in that one direction, other choices are making him turn closer and closer to Satan and turning back becomes more and more challenging. Soon, we will be following a straight path to Satan. It is never impossible to get back to following God, but it always easier if you make the right turn in the first place. Although you may see it as just one sin, that sin may turn you in the direction of many others. Where we are right now in our life, is the result of all the uncountable number of choices that we have made thus far. Our lives have been a constant change in the turns toward the directions of good and evil. To God looking down, we must look like zigzagged lines. However, in your life you should come to the point where you: "Trust in the Lord with all your heart and lean not on your own understanding; in all ways acknowledge Him, and He will make your paths straight. (Proverbs 3:5,6)"

If Jesus were in your shoes at this exact moment, would he have made the same decisions that you have made thus far today? Would his plans for the rest of this week be any different? How many choices would be different, how many do you think would be the same?

God gave you your life, you must make the **choices** on how you are going to live it.

God gave life through the Son, you must make the **choice** to accept it.

God gave you the Bible to show all the right choices, you must make the **choice** to follow its commands.

So what is your life? It is your choice?

Psalm 119:58,59 I have sought your face with all my heart; be gracious to me according to your promise. I have considered my ways and have turned my steps to your statutes.

Psalm 119:133 Direct my footsteps according to your word; let no sin rule over me.

Proverbs 4:13 Hold on to instruction, do not let it go; guard it well, for it is your life.

Ephesians 5:11 Have nothing to do with the fruitless deeds of darkness, but rather expose them.

Philippians 1:9 And this is my prayer: that your love may abound more and more in knowledge and depth of insight

The Christian's Test

The following is a test of 12 "could you" questions that you answer to determine what kid of a Christian you are. So answer them honestly and check the scoring guide at the bottom to see how you did.

#1 Could you still focus of worshipping God if you did not eat for a week or went 2 days without sleep?

#2 Could you still follow Jesus even if all your friends gave up Christianity, and they ridiculed you for keeping your faith?

#3 Could you follow Jesus if you lived in a land where no one believed in God and punished everyone that did? (More Love to Thee devotional)

#4 Could you say no to a large amount of money because you knew it was wrong, like Walter May's decision to give up a million $ in order to accuse the wrong man of a crime? (Do everything as Jesus Would devotional)

#5 Could you tell another how to be a Christian if they asked you?

#6 Could you take a bullet for a friend that you loved, risking your own life for theirs?

#7 Could you still praise God if you lost all your money and everything you had, like Job did in the Bible?

#8 Could you forgive a thought-to-be friend that went behind your back telling many awful things about you that were not true?

#9 Could you still worship God even if you were beaten, mocked, and tortured like Jesus was during the hours before his death?

#10 Could you love another as yourself to a person such as a murderer who had killed a family member or close friend? (Forgiveness devotional)

#11 Could you tell me where in the Bible to find such things like the 10 commandments, the sermon on the mount, the fruits of the spirit, and the David and Goliath story?

#12 Could you say for 100% that you would go to heaven if you were to die right now?

The results: Well, this test was not one of those test that if you got a 10-12 right you are a super Christian, 6-10 a good Christian, etc. In all actuality, all of these questions except the last one really do not matter. The only question you have to ask is "Is Jesus Christ in my heart?" For then we know the answer to #12.

As for God concerns, if life were a test you either get a 100 or a 0. There is no in between. You either worship God or you worship something else in this world. Yes, God would love it if you could honestly say yes to all these questions, but no one truly can – we all are as guilty of sin as the next guy. But, if you love the Lord Jesus Christ with all you heart, soul, mind, and strength, you can be assured 100% that you are going to heaven.

As for all of these twelve question I asked you, good if you could honestly say "yes" to some of them, but if you could not do not worry. It will become easier to do after you seek to know and love God more. If you truly commit yourselves to God and love him with all or heart like you say, you will slowly grow into the Christian that will make these Christ-like decisions. However, we will never get there by trying to make the right decisions each day. For trying to make the right decisions will never get us anywhere; we all will sin and that strategy will quickly fail.

We may never really notice the change of becoming more like Christ until long after it has happened. Because, we become a better

Christian when we try to love God more. It is not one thing you do or a specific time you have to do it that makes you closer to God, but it is the love in your heart that will make the difference. But just by loving Him you will want to become more like Christ - you will make the right decision unconsciously; you will make the choices which "turns" you to God; and you will become closer and closer to Him.

Let me finish by asking you one more "could you" question.

Could you not love the God that loved you so much that He died the painful death on the cross so that you may have paradise?

If you love God, the choice of doing right will follow.

Mark 12:30 Love the Lord your God with all your heart and with all your soul and with all your mind and with all your strength.

I John 4:17 In this way, love is made complete among us so that we will have confidence on the day of judgment, because in this world we are like him.

I Peter 4:5,6 But they will have to give account to him who is ready to judge the living and the dead. For this is the reason the gospel was preached even to those who are now dead, so that they might be judged according to men in regard to the body, but live according to God in regard to the spirit.

Romans 14:12 So then, each of us will give an account of himself to God.

Assembling the Body of Christ

Henry Ford was born to a farming family in the state of Michigan. Henry quickly found out that he did not like farming; his passion was for building things. In his childhood days, he played with blocks and built homes with Lincoln logs. During his teenage years, he moved on to fixing watches, repairing appliances, and taking things apart just to see how they worked. In his early twenties, Ford landed a job making a combustible gasoline-powered engine for an automobile. Before long, the gas-powered engines quickly became more popular than its steam and battery operated competition. Ford, being a pioneer in the gas-powered industry, rose to the top of the ladder in the field. However, it was not the engine that would make Henry Ford an American icon, but it was his invention of the assembly line that brought him his fame. Instead of having his factory workers to work together in groups to build an automobile from top to bottom, Ford introduced a process that allowed for one person to be responsible for putting together just one part. A team of about thirty would take their one part, do their job, and eventually would make up the whole car. They simply had to assemble their one part, as these parts of the unfinished car moved along the assembly line. This idea revolutionized the automobile industry, as well as factory production around the globe. The process allowed for the production of cars at about 5 times the speed of the old way. Under Ford's leadership, the company grew to be one of the greatest automobile companies of the world, and it still remains today as one of the major automobile manufactures in the world.

Though the assembly line was a great idea from Ford; he did not invent it. For the principle has been around for years. For example, the way a colony of bees work together. Or even better, what the Bible calls us to do for the kingdom of God.

In the Bible, it calls us believers to be the body of Christ. While none of us can individually put together a display that impacts the whole world, together we can.

Each and every one of us has been given special talents to do that one thing that will add to that one main "production." Some of us have a gift of teaching, others have speaking, others can learn a new language and witness to other nations, some can write/teach theology about the Law, others work great with children, some are blessed with leadership, some are blessed with determination to become anything they put their mind to, others have been giving a willingness to serve, some are talented musically, some are good listeners, and some are good examples. Regardless if you think you are talented or blessed, you have something that you can contribute to the Body of Christ.

So what should be that one thing or things that you contribute? Find what it is that you truly love (not because of self-centered reasons like it is easy, but where your heart seems to want to be). Try doing several projects for the Church/community and find what it is that best fits you. Ask others to see what they think would be best for you to do, to impact the world. And do not forget to pray to God to ask him for direction, or pray that your talents may be manifest in whatever way He wants.

The two best things for one to do for the further meant of God's kingdom is – 1)the willingness to serve and 2) the ability to love. These two things any person can do, and these two closely related things have the biggest impact for Christianity. In everything we do, these two things should be evident in our words, actions, and deeds. Serving and loving is what being the Body of Christ is all about.

As the smallest member of the body of Christ we are like cells that make up the human body. We are called to function in a particular way in order to form a larger body. Using our metaphor of the body, our cell would contribute with other like cells, to make up a tissue, our tissue to an organ, our organ to a system, and finally our system to the body. We must constantly be working together to do that one little thing to make up our microscopic part that makes up the Body?

I am sure you get the picture of how it works, but what are you giving to the body. You may know your talents; you may have the time; but many of us still waste our resources. How can the body function if its cells do not do what they are supposed to do? In the human body, a cell that exists but does not function is called a cancer. If you are not doing anything for God, you are not functioning as a cell. Are you a cancer on the body of Christ?

The popular Christian music group Casting Crowns takes up the topic of not functioning in the Body of Christ in one of their famous songs in which they sing,

> "But if we are the body
> Why aren't His arms reaching?
> Why aren't His hands healing?
> Why aren't His words teaching?
> And if we are the body
> Why aren't His feet going?
> Why is His love not showing them there is a way?" [1]

Today, take some time to find where God wants you to go. God has a plan for you.

You may have Christ in you, but is your body making up the body of Christ?

I Corinthians 12:12 The body is a unit, though it is made up of many parts; and though all its parts are many, they form one body. So it is with Christ.

I Corinthians 12:27-31 Now you are the body of Christ, and each one of you is a part of it. And in the church God has appointed first of all apostles, second prophets, third teachers, then workers of miracles, also those having gifts of healing, those able to help others, those with gifts of administration, and those speaking in different kinds of tongues. Are all apostles? Are all prophets? Are all teachers? Do all work miracles? Do all have gifts of healing? Do all speak in tongues? Do all interpret? But eagerly desire the greater gifts.

Ecclesiastes 9:10 Whatever your hand finds to do, do it with all your might, for in the grave, where you are going, there is neither working nor planning nor knowledge nor wisdom.

Ephesians 4:7,8 But to each one of us grace has been given as Christ apportioned it. This is why it says: "When he ascended on high, he led captives in his train and gave gifts to men."

Ephesians 5:17 Therefore do not be foolish, but understand what the Lord's will is

Romans 9:20 But who are you, O man, to talk back to God? "Shall what is formed say to him who formed it, `Why did you make me like this?' "

Romans 12:5 so in Christ we who are many form one body, and each member belongs to all the others. We have different gifts, according to the grace given us. If a man's gift is prophesying, let him use it in proportion to his faith. If it is serving, let him serve; if it is teaching, let him teach; if it is encouraging, let him encourage; if it is contributing to the needs of others, let him give generously; if it is leadership, let him govern diligently; if it is showing mercy, let him do it cheerfully

---

[1] Source: "If We Are the Body." Casting Crowns. 2003

Where is God in your life...

The plans were set; the arrangements were made; and everyone was ready for spring break 2000. For weeks, Luke Webber had been looking forward to putting away the books and forgetting all his responsibilities, in order to do whatever he wanted at the beautiful beeches of Fort Lauderdale. At lunch one day, a group of Luke's friends were talking of their great trips of years past and what they were going to do this year for their spring vacation. In the middle of their talks, Luke noticed Danny Archie excluded from the conversation. Luke and Danny were not the greatest friends, but he knew that Danny did not have any friends to go on spring break with, so Luke asked him, "Hey Danny, you aren't going anywhere for spring break are you?" "Well, um-" Luke interrupted, "My Aunt has a place down in Fort Lauderdale and a couple of us guys are going, you can come along if you want." "Sure," he quickly responded, "if that's ok with you guys."

Early that Saturday morning, Luke and Danny loaded up their stuff in Luke's SUV, and headed out on their 12-hour ride from Xavier, Ohio. Unfortunately this ride only lasted about 15 minutes. Twenty miles out of town, Luke's car crashed head first into a semi-truck whose driver had fallen asleep at the wheel. Danny, wearing his seatbelt, was able to walk away with a few scratches, but Luke was not as fortunate. Luke was rushed to the hospital with Danny being at his side in the ambulance. But before the ambulance was able to reach its destination, Luke had already passed away.

Danny took Luke's death as hard as anybody else in the community. The week of partying and having fun turned into times of sorrow – with Danny asking himself "Why?" "Why did this have to happen?" Danny began to believe that the tragedy was his fault, and he never should have been there in the first place. He went to the Webber house to apologize. The mother just tried to comfort him. "It's not your fault Danny, the Lord sometimes works in ways we never will understand. Wait right there, Danny, I want to show you something." Mrs. Webber came back with Luke's journal. "He wrote about you the night before the accident."

Danny read: "I'm so ready to take a break; school's been tough this year, having some fun on the beach is what I need. Danny Archie is coming with me. I'm glad, he seems to be a great guy, but I don't know if he really knows God all that well. We'll have a 12-hour ride down there, so I hope I can talk about God with him…." Reading this only hurt Danny even more.

Danny would sit alongside the road looking at the wooden cross, as he thought about what happened. A week later, Danny was still taking it pretty hard. At first, he could not make it to Luke's funeral, but he eventually decide on going, so he showed up late. Danny went up to Luke's mother and asked if it would be okay if he said something at the graveside service, and the crying mother agreed. After a pastor had said a great eulogy for the young man, Danny would get up in front of the large crowd and say:

"Hi, my name is Danny Archie and I was with Luke in the time of the accident. I should not of been there; I should not have been the one who lived.

This past week I have been left asking a lot of questions. The other day while starring at the wooden cross on the side of the road in honor of Luke, I wrote:

Danny then took out a folded piece of notebook and paper and read:

'Where Is God in your Life?

Is He in your heart?

Is He in your actions, words, and thoughts?

Is He the home you return to everyday to seek peace form this chaotic world?

Is He the one you are following so close behind?

Is His name written on your hands and his symbol worn around you neck?

Is He in the prayer around the dinner table?

Is He distracting you in your time to yourself, or is your time for yourself distracting you from Him?

Is He in that dusty old Bible at home?

Is He in the church you attend every Sunday?

Is He in those pictures and scriptures hanging around your house?

Is He stored up back in your closet knowing where It is, but not using It only until you have to?

Do you even consider Him living with you in your house?

Is He there wishing you goodnight each night and waking you up every morning?

Is He their lifting you up in times of sorrow?

Is He their celebrating with you in times of joy?

Is He in your free time?

Is He in you when you sing songs of praises unto His name?

Is He your Alpha and Omega?

Is He in your dreams of the future?

Is He planned somewhere in your week's agenda?

Is He seen by others within you?

Is He loved by you with all your heart, soul, mind, and strength?

For me, God is at the cross alongside the road.'

The reason I was asked to go with Luke that day was so Luke could tell me about Christ. He never mentioned one word about

God, Jesus, or the Bible on that 15-minute ride, but he has taught me so much after the ride. I lived my life going to Church, going to a Christian school, being raised by Christian parents, and living what I called a "good" life. But nowhere could you find God in my life. I knew the scripture, knew what it took to be a Christian, but He wasn't there. However what Luke wanted to show me, I found this past week. No one except Jesus Christ will ever have as much of an impact on someone else's life after their death, than what Luke has had on me. I could only imagine what Luke could have done if he were alive right now. The world has truly lost one of its best."

Right now, reread Danny's *"Where is God in your Life?"* questions, and apply them to your life.

Ask yourself, do you need more of God in your life? All of us do not have someone like Luke; we must realize on our own that we need to know God more.

Deuteronomy 6:4-6 Hear, O Israel: The LORD our God, the LORD is one. Love the LORD your God with all your heart and with all your soul and with all your strength. These commandments that I give you today are to be upon your hearts.

Exodus 15:2 The LORD is my strength and my song; he has become my salvation. He is my God, and I will praise him, my father's God, and I will exalt him.

Psalm 90:1,2 Lord, you have been our dwelling place throughout all generations. Before the mountains were born or you brought forth the earth and the world, from everlasting to everlasting you are God.

Galatians 3:9 So those who have faith are blessed along with Abraham, the man of faith

Eye Efforts

Frederick Abraham Lewis III was a young man from Panama City, FL. Abe's family had a heritage of flying planes in the air force. His father and uncles flew in Vietnam, his grandfather served in World War II, and his great grandfather flew in World War I. Carrying his great grandfather's name and having a dad who loved the air force, Abe grew up always wanting to be a pilot. On special occasions, his father got to take Abe up in a fighter jet with him on some of his required training hours. Abe dreamed of one day flying these amazing machines on his own. While other kids wanted to be sports stars, firemen, etc., Abe always wanted to be a pilot. Abe would collect aircraft toys, build model airplanes, and even make paper airplanes in class.

Terrible news came to Abe at age 15. At school during a vision and hearing check, the nurse found that Abe had 20/100 vision in both eyes and would need glasses. It was not looking nerdy that Abe worried about, but it was the fact, that to be a pilot in the air force, you had to have almost perfect vision. And Abe's 20/100 vision was well short from the required 20/70. Abe did not get glasses hoping that if he did not, maybe his vision would one day get better on its own. But it did not; it would actually get worse. At graduation, Abe's 20/200 vision could barely see the big *E* on the eye chart; the five lines under the *E* were not even visible to the squinting Abe. Abe still tried to get into the Air Force Academy as a pilot.

He tried everything to get in - He tried to tell the truth, to see for just this once if they would make an exemption, but the academy strictly enforced their rules and said that there are no exceptions. He tried using his family name, but it would not have mattered if he were the son of the president, because a rule is a rule and there is no getting around it. Then he tried lying saying that he had good vision, but this did not get him too far because the eye test is first in the physical examination after the height and weight check. He tried to wear contacts, but they were spotted. He tried memorizing the eye chart, which would have worked, if the nurse did not tell him to read it backwards. He tried everything, but he could do nothing.

One day Abe went to his eye doctor, to refill a contact subscription, when he asked the doctor if there was any way to improve his eyesight naturally, even for just a little while. The doctor remembered, while in optometrist school, of a guy who said that after a series of eye exercises called optametrics, that one's vision could steadily increase. He said, "there is no evidence that it works, but it is used by doctors is India and third world countries whose patients can not afford glasses. It's kind of a witch doctor trick for the eye, but I guess you could give it a shot." So, Abe would go on to buy the book *Training you Eye: Reshaping your Vision* by Dr. Benow**. For over an hour a day, Abe would "workout" his eyes by quickly moving them up and down, bouncing them from side to side, looking up close then far away, looking out of the corner of his eye, and doing all sorts of funny looking techniques. After 3½ years of effort each day, Abe was able to improve his eyesight to that required by the Air Force. Abe was able to live out his dream by being a pilot in the First Gulf War.

**Today, Optametrics is no longer used. With techniques such as LASIK eye surgery, Optometrics (except for third world countries) has now become outdated. However athletes such as baseball players have added Abe's routine in their training regimen, claiming it gives them better hand eye coordination along with helping them to better to pick up an object, such as a ball.

After years of trying and hours of effort, Abe was finally able to find a way to get passed that impossible object and reach his dream. Too many of us have that impossible object blocking us in our life. In these things, we must trust God and try with great effort to do what seems impossible. Remember, nothing is impossible with God.

For many of us, that impossible object is sin. Some claim that some sins cannot be avoided and are just a part of who we are. People say that things like drugs, lying, and homosexuality are naturally a part of who they are - that they were born being a person who cannot resist these things. But I can promise you, that even though you may have been born a "crack baby," you were not meant to be a drug addict; while you find it natural to lie, this does not mean that you should constantly lie; and even though you may have all the characteristics and are attracted to the same sex, you were not created to be a homosexual. Some argue this saying, "They are just sins – we all sin. By God's grace, all sins can be washed away." True, we are told in the Bible that we are saved by God's grace, but it also calls us to love. Jesus said that the most important thing we can do is this: "Love the Lord your God with all your heart and with all your soul and with all your mind and with all your strength. The second is this: Love your neighbor as yourself. There is no commandment greater then these." Mark 12:29

If you love God, then you should have no troubles giving up your life of sin. If you say that you love God, but cannot give up the sin – you are just loving the sin more than you love God.

Others will struggle with certain sins more than others. For those who have a strong inclination toward a sin, they must try everything and give a great effort, like Abe, in order to reach a seemingly impossible task. I encourage you to get someone who cares to help you or keep you accountable (close friend, spouse, church leader), or maybe seek professional help to keep you away from a sin that can dominate your life. Sure you may be willing to quit your particular sin now, but if you are truly inclined to a particular sin, within three days these words I have told you, will have left; and the feeling you have right now, will not be the same. The result would be for you to going back to that one sin. But do not let this be; make it your priority to keep this sin away from you. It may not seem like you will ever reach your task, but if you love God, you will.

So what is that one sin in your life – drugs, alcohol, lying, pornography, pride, greed, homosexuality? Today start to give up that sin. Find someone or a program that keeps you accountable, write down the time and cause of your struggles/temptations, and give that extra effort to do whatever is needed to get that sin out of your life. The only advice I can give to you is: To remember God's love, and let that love inspire you to give the effort that is needed to reach that impossible goal.

With love, anything is a possibility, and there is always a way.

2 Peter 1:4 Through these he has given us his very great and precious promises, so that through them you may participate in the divine nature and escape the corruption in the world caused by evil desires.
Psalm 119:30,31 I have chosen the way of truth; I have set my heart on your laws. I hold fast to your statutes, O LORD; do not let me be put to shame.

Psalm 119:115 Away from me, you evildoers, that I may keep the commands of my God!
Hebrews 12:1 Therefore, since we are surrounded by such a great cloud of witnesses, let us throw off everything that hinders and the sin that so easily entangles, and let us run with perseverance the race marked out for us
1 John 2:17 The world and its desires pass away, but the man who does the will of God lives forever.
2 John 6 And this is love: that we walk in obedience to his commands. As you have heard from the beginning, his command is that you walk in love.
James 4:17 Anyone, then, who knows the good he ought to do and doesn't do it, sins.

A Fairytale of Love

Once upon a time there was a man named Marc Carey. Marc was a 24-year-old gentlemen from Redwood, California. In the summer of 2000, while he was working as a lifeguard on the beach, Marc met a beautiful girl named Katherine. He found himself very attracted to this 22-year-old college student. Although they had only talked a couple of times on the beach and had dinner together one night, Katherine seemed to be the perfect match for him. Mark felt so close to this girl. He found himself falling in love. At night before going to sleep, he would dream of times of being together with Katherine in the future. During the day on the lifeguard stand, he would long just to be with her. As he watched couples together at the beach, he pictured Katherine and him together in future days. He could not explain this felling called love inside of him. Love made him do things when he was around her that Mr. Serious would have never done before. He knew that he would do anything for this girl. However, Katherine did not share the same feelings. When it was time for her to leave, Mark did not want to say good-bye. He told Katherine that he wanted to come down to visit the college campus to visit her. He told her of his whimsical idea that she could move to the Redwood area with him after her graduation. Katherine just gave a half-hearted smile and said, "Well, you have it all planned out." Katherine had an uneasy feeling listening to Marc, as she was thinking in her head of a way to tell him that there was someone back at UCLA that she had been dating for two years. She just wanted to tell him that even though she had a great time with him, she never thought anything would ever become serious between them. But she could not find the words to tell him this.

As Katherine was getting ready to drive back to Los Angeles, Mark held her hand and walked her out to her car. There, he told her that he loved her. Katherine just looked at Marc's innocent eyes shaking her head saying, "I'm sorry Mark, I just don't feel this way about you." Then she drove off, leaving this heartbroken man behind.

Mark tried to move on, but he knew deep down inside that he still loved this girl. The two did stay in touch over time, talking on the phone and sending emails. Mark would always mention the idea of them together, even offering to move to where she started her career. But Katherine would just ignore Marc's wishful thinking of them together, and she would always quickly change the subject.

A year and a half later, Katherine decided one day that having someone who really cared for her was what see needed in her life, now that she had graduated college. So, Katherine decided to visit Marc in Redwood for a week. Over that week, Katherine started to enjoy Marc's attempts to win her love, and she began to start to have feelings for Marc. After a year of dating, the two would get married in St. Louis, Missouri, where they have since moved and lived happily ever after.

Here we see what love can make a person feel and do. When we love someone in this type of way, a person will do anything for that person; they will do things that they never would have before, and they experience a great joy with just being with that person.

Have you experienced this feeling with God?

When we experience this love, we experience the joys of being a Christian. I write over love more than any other subject, because love is the heart of what God is all about. The trouble is that I cannot explain this feeling to you in words. Love cannot be bottled up or sold at a price, but love is something that is shared; it is something we can give; it's an experience we want so badly but cannot explain why; it is the greatest thing that man can have in this world. This feeling is something all Christians should know all to well. For it is by God's love that made you into the person that you are today. And the more we love this Thing, the more that we find that It loves us back. Unlike Katherine, who would not commit to a loving relationship, God will never spare His love for us. He has loved us for all-time, and He will continue to love us no matter how many times we break His heart.

Love is also unselfish and serving. As Marc was willing to do anything for the girl that he loved, we too should be willing to do anything for God – and actually enjoy doing it. Marc cherished just to be around Katherine; he absolutely enjoyed doing something for the one he loved. Look at Jesus, the perfect example of love. Look what all he did for us. He did not show his love to his followers by giving them riches or joyous experiences. He showed his love by giving to, doing for, and serving others. The ultimate example of love is when Jesus gave everything he had, by enduring the pain of the cross.

Also, there is not a set mark for you to measure your love, or a way to know how to show your love. Like in a dating relationship, there is no test to decide whether you are in love – you just know. And when you are in love, there is no book that is needed to tell you what to do – you simply know how to express your feelings.

With God, we never know an amount or level of our love – we simply know if we are in love, or if our love is not where it should be. For the ones that love Him, they know how to love Him. All Christians can figure out how to show our love (doing right, praying with a thankful heart, etc.) It is not a mystery how you should show your love, because you know the ways that you can personally love Him best.

Finding ways to show our love is not the hard part; it is finding this love inside us that allows us to show this love that should be our concern.

If someone saw Marc and Katherine in love, would that same person see this love or a greater love between you and God?

Has your love for God compelled you to do something for Him and enjoy it?

Has it made you do things that you would not have done for anything or anybody else? Has it made you do things that you never thought possible?

Does it give you complete joy when you are with Him?

Have you totally found this love?

If you have the love of God, you can be assured that you will live a life happily ever after.

Song of Solomon 8:6b, 7 For love is as strong as death, its jealousy unyielding as the grave. It burns like blazing fire, like a mighty flame. Many waters cannot quench love; rivers cannot wash it away.

Ephesians 5:2 live a life of love, just as Christ loved us and gave himself up for us as a fragrant offering and sacrifice to God.

I Corinthians 13:8a Love never fails.

I John 4:16 And so we know and rely on the love God has for us. God is love. Whoever lives in love lives in God, and God in him

A Childlike Heart

Amy Avery went to the doctor for what was thought to be a normal cold. However, the 13-year-old girl soon found out that her flu-like symptoms was a result of a rare type of leukemia in which she was not producing enough blood. The doctor warned Amy's mother, that if things did not get better that her young daughter's condition could result in death. For any treatments to be attempted, a large donation of a perfect match of blood was needed. The closest match found was Amy's seven-year-old brother, Timmy. It just so happened that little Timmy had an extreme fear of shots and needles, even for a child his age. However, once Timmy's mother explained to him that it was for his sister, Timmy let his parents take him to the hospital where he would give his blood. Timmy sat on the cold stool shaking with fear waiting for the doctor. The doctor, knowing Timmy's fear, tried to make the little boy comfortable, so before taking out any needles or tubes, he tried to start a conversation with little Timmy. As the doctor was asking Timmy what his favorite color was, Timmy interrupted and asked, "How long after I get my shots will I die?" The doctor compelled by little Timmy's statement replied, "Timmy you certainly won't die. You may not feel good for a day or two, but you won't die." The doctor stopped and then sat down beside the boy to tell the boy actually what he would be doing. "You see Timmy, we are just going to take a little of your blood by using this needle, so that we can give it to your sister, because her blood, right now, is making her sick."

The doctor thought to himself for a second and asked, "Timmy, why would you give your blood if you thought you would die?'

Timmy responded, "Because I love Sissy. I would do anything to make her better."

This little boy showed the greatest example of love by what he was he willing to do - or at least what he thought he had to do. Jesus had this love inside of him when he willingly lay down his life on the cross to save us from the disease of sin, which causes our death.

Do you have this love inside you?

A child's love is one like none other. While a child can sometimes be very self-centered, a child can also have one of the best senses of love. Children have not yet experienced all the evil in this world; they have not been marred from sins like greed over money, obsessions on sex, depression from not reaching your dreams, and many of the other terrible things of this world. This is why they have one of the purest senses of love. In Timmy's sense, he would give his own life for that he loved. Jesus said, "Greater love has no one than this, that he lay down his life for his friends."(John 15:17) Somewhere in the talks of death, how Timmy was needed for his sister, and what Timmy had in his mind about shots and needles - Timmy thought that he was going to be the one who had to lay down his life for his [sister]. Even at age young age, love can make humans do remarkable things.

We all long to be like children: when our greatest joy was seeing Daddy come in from work in the afternoon; or when we woke up on summer mornings, knowing we did not have anything to do that day but play with friends and eat popsicles when we got too hot; or when we did not have a care in the world, but had a love for everything from cartoons to Grandma's chocolate chip cookies. People long deep down to be a child because they long for this love that they had during this time. While there is no fountain of youth or time machine to turn back your age to this great time, there is a means by which we can get this feeling that we long for. That feeling is God. We as people long to be loved and to love. And we find God as the ultimate object to satisfy both of these desires. We need God, and we want God.

When Jesus said that our love should be childlike, I think that this is what he meant. He wanted us to have a pure love not jaded by evil and sin. He wanted us to be like little Timmy whose love was greater than his own life.

You have love in your life, but is it this kind of love?

We all long for it, but have you discovered that God is the only way to satisfy this feeling that all humans share?

Matthew 18:3,4 And he said:"I tell you the truth, unless you change and become like little children, you will never enter the kingdom of heaven. Therefore, whoever humbles himself like this child is the greatest in the kingdom of heaven.

Luke 18:17 I tell you the truth, anyone who will not receive the kingdom of God like a little child will never enter it.

John 15:12,13 My command is this: Love each other as I have loved you. Greater love has no one than this, that he lay down his life for his friends.

I John 3:1 How great is the love the Father has lavished on us, that we should be called children of God! And that is what we are!

Forgiveness

Donavan Monroe received a phone call late one night at 3:00 in the morning. Over the line, was a police officer notifying Donavan that his daughter Meredith had been found dead on the streets. He mentioned that they had evidence of foul play.

Donavan was in shock; he did know if this was for real or if he was dreaming. His wife rolled over and asked, "Don, what is it?" Tears began streaming down his face as his lips quivered to tell his wife, "It's our baby girl, she's dead."

Donavan called up his parents to look after their 14 and 11 year old sons, and he and his wife left to the hospital. There the police told them in detail of what they believed was the cause of her death. They suspected that Meredith was a rape victim that was killed by her attacker after the assault. There were several witnesses including three of Meredith's friends that saw Meredith at a Jazz club that night. No one saw her leave the club, but after midnight, she was nowhere to be found. The police officer said that forensic scientists would do the best they could with the evidence they had, to catch the attacker. The police had to ask Donavon just to take a look at the body to confirm that it was his daughter. As the coroner pulled back the bed sheet, Donavan saw that it was his daughter, and he could not bare to look at it a second longer. The beautiful 24-year-old's body was covered in deep cuts and large bruises. Donavan had this in his mind as his last picture of what he would see of his daughter.

The whole family took Meredith's death hard, and Donavan probably took it the hardest. He could not believe that this could happen to his baby girl. She had just set out into the world moving into her first apartment just 9 months ago; it seemed like only yesterday that she was kissing him goodnight after he read her a bedtime story; it seemed only a short time ago when he had to hold her hand, walking her into kindergarten. He hated having to say good-bye to her when she left for college; now he was having to say good-bye forever.

A week later, the same policeman called the Monroe house and said that they had caught Meredith's alleged killer. It turned out to be a twenty-year-old boy. The police said that they had more than enough substantial evidences to attain the boy. The boy's fingerprints and DNA were all over the body. Meredith's three friends were asked to look at the line up of several men, to see if they recognized any from the jazz club that night. All of them picked out that same twenty-year-old guy, saying that they remember him because he gave them an uncomfortable stare as they walked in the door.

Donavan decided to confront this kid, even though the police did not recommend it.

"Son, do you realize what you have done to me," Donavan said as he paced in front of the jail cell, "you've taken the blessing I would give my life for, you have taken the big sister of two boys that loved Meredith to death; my wife cannot get out of bed because she is so upset."

The boy looked up and stared Donavan right in the eye and said, "You must be that B———'s father."

The policemen had to restrain Donavan as he grabbed the young man by the collar. Donavan left in a bitter rage.

Donavan's anger only grew the more he thought about it. He could not sleep; his thoughts were of memories of his daughter, mixed with hate for this guy who took it all away from him. He let his anger get out of control.

However, Donavon knew that he could not harbor up this anger, so he went to the confessional to talk to his priest. He explained the situation to the priest.

The priest said, "there is nothing you can do now, my son. You must forgive the man and leave it to the law and God to convict this man."

"But father, it was the way he smarted off to me, the way my daughter looked after her death, the way I had to receive that phone call that turned my world upside down – these things I will never forget."

"As your Father has forgiven you, you likewise should forgive."

"It's not that easy. Sure I could forgive him if he say backed into my car and dented its front end, but he disrespected my daughter; he took away my little girl."

The priest suggested several passages out of the Bible for Donavan to read.

After reading the passages and hearing the priest's words, Donavan was ready to give some sort of apology, even though he did not do anything. However, he wanted to clear his conscience and let go of the anger stored inside of him. But when he returned to the jail, the police officer said that the boy's well-to-do doctor father had paid the highly expensive bail, and the boy was free until his trial next month. Donavan's anger began to build, but he still wanted to do right, so he looked up where the boy lived and visited his apartment.

As the boy opened the door, Donavan swallowed his throat and said, "Son, I forgive you for what you did to my daughter, I pray that you will know God who is the only one that can wipe away...."

The boy, who was laughing, interrupted, "Forgive me, what did I do?" "My father's got the best lawyers in the city; he will get me out of this just like he got me out of jail."

Donavan gritted his teeth, and swung his fist as hard as he could at the boy's face. The boy moved his head and Donavan's knuckles went crashing through the wall. Donavan took his other hand and grabbed the boy by the neck. As the boy was chocking for air, Donavan realized what he was doing and slowly let go. He glared at the boy for several seconds and finally turned around and left.

After that day, Donavan would struggle countless times to forgive this individual who had caused so much pain in his life. Two years later before the boy's execution, Donavan was able to go up to him, look him in the eye, and say that he forgave him. It was a task harder than anything else Donavan had ever done. But as much as he loved Christ, he could not stand the thought of God not forgiving him – so he knew that he could at least forgive this one person.

As you can see with Donavan example, not being able to forgive others produces hatred inside of us. Hatred is the exact opposite of love. Where love allows us to do great things; hate leads to sin. Unforgiving is to hate as forgiveness is to love. This is why forgiveness is one of the central ideas of what Christianity is all about.

We have heard all the quotes, "forgive others, as God had forgiven you," and "love others as yourself." But can you do it? What would you have done in Donavan's situation?

There will always be strife in this world. A lot of times it is not our fault, but the shortcomings/pain falls on us. Just look at the world today – neighbors build fences because they cannot get along with the one next door, people driving cars are always yelling and arguing at another whose driving skills they have a problem with, and in the news there are always terrorists attacks between two nations that are bitter enemies. It makes one want to say, "Why can't we all just get along."

Forgiving others is included in Christ's universal message of loving others.

We harbor bitterness because we do no like what others say or do, but how is this different from our own self? What I mean by this is: I am sure you do not like what you do sometimes: people embarrass themselves in what we say; we let ourselves down by not doing what we want to do; and we are not always happy with what we have done with ourselves. But that never stopped us from getting along with our self and forgiving our own self. We are all different

- we are bound not to like what others say and do, but we should not let this stop us from loving and forgiving them.

Our problem with forgiving, is that our society is bent too much on a revenge attitude. When someone wrongs us; we wrong them. When this process happens, the little things will escalate until hate develops. I've seen things like - not paying back twenty dollars, parking a car in someone else's yard, dropping a notebook that caused another's papers to get scattered, and helping someone by cutting their grass - tear people apart. Sure, it's not unnatural for people to get mad, but for such things to cause such trouble, there is no sense. As a Christian, you should seek forgiveness in some way. Whether it calls for a formal apology or a way for you to show that you are not harboring any bitterness toward that person, you should find a means to love others as yourself. For example, if you were a guy that grew to hate another guy for a reason like mentioned above, try starting a conversation about a common interest, such as sports. Talk about that a couple minutes and at a good time mention something like, "Hey man, I am sorry for the other day, I do not know why I do that kind of thing." A lot of times, you have to be the one to take initiative to forgive first, whether it is your fault or not.

I will go ahead and warn you that there is a lot of people who will not accept an apology; there are a lot of people who will not forgive you no matter how the small the matter; there are those who will continue to wrong you even if you have sought forgiveness; and there are a lot of people who are just plain evil and will continue to wrong/hate you no matter if you have forgiven them or not.

For those who do not accept the apology, be persistent in showing kindness to them; for showing love to others will effect them in some way; it just may take more love or more time for some to come around.

For those who keep wronging you, even if it is doing the same thing over and over again, you must continually be forgiving them. Jesus said that you should not forgive someone just seven times but 7 times 77. It can grow frustrating to forgive someone for the same thing over and over again, but all that you can do is set up something to prevent them from doing wrong to you, while at same time showing them that your life is full of love.

And for those that are just pure evil, you are also called to forgive them. Nowhere in the Bible does it give an exception to not to forgive someone. You never know, showing love and forgiveness has caused some of the most unlikely converts to Christianity (many of which stories are in my other devotionals).

So think right now, is there anyone that you are harboring anger against deep down inside?

Is there anyone that you need to forgive?

God forgives the millions of sins we commit in our lifetimes. He forgave us by showing his love by dying on the Cross.

So why do we find it so hard to show love for others by forgiving them?

Ephesians 4:32 Be kind and compassionate to one another, forgiving each other, just as in Christ God forgave you.

Romans 12:20,21 If your enemy is hungry, feed him; if he is thirsty, give him something to drink. In doing this, you will heap burning coals on his head." Do not be overcome by evil, but overcome evil with good.

Luke 6:27, 37 "But I tell you who hear me: Love your enemies, do good to those who hate you,

Do not judge, and you will not be judged. Do not condemn, and you will not be condemned. Forgive, and you will be forgiven

Matthew 18:21,22 Then Peter came to Jesus and asked, "Lord, how many times shall I forgive my brother when he sins against me? Up to seven times?"

Jesus answered, "I tell you, not seven times, but seventy-seven times.

Matthew 6:14,15 For if you forgive men when they sin against you, your heavenly Father will also forgive you. But if you do not forgive men their sins, your Father will not forgive your sins.

Being Humble

William Ralston was a wealthy businessman that lived in the 1800's. At an early age, William moved out West to look for a job on the thriving west coast. William's charm and likable character landed him a job with a railroad company. And before long William became one of the men to make it rich off the railroad. William ended up building a large mansion for him and his family in Belmont, CA (this building is now one of the main buildings on the Notre Dame campus). William loved the process of building houses, so he started to give part of his time, in order to start communities along the railroad. One of his communities quickly grew and before long its population qualified it to be considered a city. Community leaders came together and wanted to name the town after its creator, Ralston – throwing out such names like Williamstown or Ralstonville. Even though the act honored William, he said that he would rather it be named after something else. But the townspeople all loved William and all he did for them. After all he contributed much of his own money to establish the community, and he was a man that was adored by the whole community. So they once again persisted that the town be named after William. But William said, "I can not accept this, I do not want to be remembered for being the establisher of this town; I want this town to be remembered for the people that has been established in it." The town leaders all respected William's humble attitude, so they came together and finally agreed the town should be named Modesto (Spanish for modest) after William's unselfish attitude. This town has grown tremendously since this time, and this thriving city still bears the mark of the humbleness of a great man.

When we hear of acts or stories of humbleness, we are touched and greatly respect that person – this is the exact opposite feeling we have towards pride. Being humble is one of the greatest qualities we as a person can show. Because when we are humble, we are thinking of others before one's self, or basically we are loving our neighbor as our self.

The reason why William Ralston was so well like was not because of his charm, money, or position in the railroad company; but he was so well liked because he was humble. I'm sure, William did not go around telling people that they were so much better than him or that he did not deserve all that he had, for that is not what is means to be humble. Rather, I think William was just that nice guy who would do things like the following: listen to anyone, help others even though he could be helping himself, take time to remember others even when he was very busy, treat all of his neighbors as equals no matter what their social class, and knowing that he was not deserving of all his praise. I suppose if you met Mr. Ralston today, you would not think to yourself, "wow, this man is really humble," but I would guess you would just see this man as a loving man that is easy to get along with.

Being humble in your spiritual lives is of greatest importance. For when we are fully humble, we recognize how much of a sinner we are. And when we realize the magnitude of our sins, two great things happen. 1) We are aware of our sins, preventing Satan to attack us to do evil, when we think we are doing nothing wrong. 2) When we recognize our sins, it makes us desire to love God more, because we see how much we have wronged him, how much we need him, and how much He loves us by welcoming a sinner like us into His family. When we are not humble, we have pride, and pride is one of the most powerful sins that ruins lives and causes one to fall from God.

Some people seem to be naturally prideful, while others may not struggle as much over it. Pride is just one of those things which some are more susceptible than others. But do not get me wrong - pride can influence all. After so many praises or awards for one's efforts, the human seems to naturally gain a sense of pride (I am guessing this is the result of the fall of man, when Adam's first sin was eating the fruit for pride into becoming like God, or back before time when Lucifer rebelled from God out of pride).

The process of pride will go something like this: we receive many praises and compliments by others, and naturally one thinks better of himself or of his works – which is not a bad thing but it will eventually lead to future problems. Next, one will spend more time thinking of himself or his work – this is when a person gets to the point where he shows his inward feelings (or pride) over himself. And finally in a short amount of time, this pride will fully develop a harmful sense of loving oneself.

I am reminded of an example of this, years ago when I had a teammate on my baseball team. He was a mediocre pitcher, and he and everyone else on the team knew that. One day he pitched the game of his life, and he got many praises from others like: "good game," "you're pitched great," and "you did wonderful out there." This seemed to make my friend start to feel good about himself. Then he went on to have two or three good games in a row, and he was receiving comments like: "you have been pitching awesome lately" and "you're one of the best pitchers I've seen." Then that person let these praises sink in. Even though he knew deep down inside that he was not as good as people made him out to be, he still began to think very highly of himself. Then this person let it get to his head; at practice, he would not do the things he used to do. At that moment in time, he rationed out that he was the star pitcher, and he did not need to spend all his time practicing hard or taking time to help others on the team. Since he was not pushing himself at practice, his pitching performances showed his lack of effort. Though he was not pitching well, he still expected the praises and cheers after every game. When he pitched terrible, he only made up excuses saying them in a manner like he was better than everyone, and it was something or someone else's fault as to why he did not have an exceptional performance. This young man's pride eventually led to him being kicked off the team for his unselfish attitude and lack of giving any effort.

Everyone has seen it; everyone has gone through it, especially in our walk with God. Sometimes (especially when we compare ourselves to others) we get a prideful sense that we are a good person. And this sense of pride is not just a sin in our thoughts, but a sin in our attitude. By being in our attitude, it is though we do not think about making the decision before we do something – we simply just act on it. Being prideful is about reacting to a certain situation, instead of having time to make a choice of right or wrong. This is why it is so important to be humble; because when we are humble, we are of the right attitude to live our lives as God called us to live in his Word.

So how do we become humble? You can wait until your pride gets so high that it causes you to fall flat on your face, making you have to get up and start over, like in the case of my teammate. However, I recommend you be in continual prayer to be humble, and examining your life to see in what ways or areas you have let pride in your life. I recommend you thinking about it now and writing it down. This way, every week or month you can be reminded of how you had pride in the past, as you write down how pride is in you at the present. This can helpful in keeping you humble and pointing out the ways in which you have developed and are developing pride.

So how humble are you?

Did you answer this question with any sense of pride?

Proverbs 27:1-2 Do not boast about tomorrow, for you do not know what a day may bring forth. Let another praise you, and not your own mouth; someone else, and not your own lips.

Romans 12:16 Live in harmony with one another. Do not be proud, but be willing to associate with people of low position. Do not be conceited

Luke 14:11 For everyone who exalts himself will be humbled, and he who humbles himself will be exalted

Romans 12:3 For by the grace given me I say to every one of you: Do not think of yourself more highly than you ought, but rather think of yourself with sober judgment, in accordance with the measure of faith God has given you.

Philippians 2:5,6 Your attitude should be the same as that of Christ Jesus:

Who, being in very nature God, did not consider equality with God something to be grasped, but made himself nothing, taking the very nature of a servant, being made in human likeness.

Proverbs 29:23 A man's pride brings him low, but a man of lowly spirit gains honor

James 4:6 But he gives us more grace. That is why Scripture says: God opposes the proud but gives grace to the humble

Revenge

Fernando Rodriguez was a boy that grew up in the Central American country of Honduras. Living in the central plains of the country, there were only two things a boy could do: work in the sugar cane fields and play baseball. In the village of Jutlcalpa, everyone was the same. Everyone either grows sugar cane or extracts the sugar from the sugar cane to export to countries like the United States. Fernando was introduced to the sugar cane fields at the age of four, where he would work for many of his days as a youth. All the kids worked anywhere from six to twelve hours days in the fields. However, when six o'clock rolled around, every kid ran to the rocky field in the middle of town to do what they looked forward to all day: to play baseball. For three hours the boys would play their hearts out, using a tattered ball and a bat that was nothing more than a stick. After returning home for a quick meal, the boys would gather at a meeting place and crowd around a tiny radio where they would listen to Major League Baseball. Men like Josẽ Guiterrez, Manuel Cruz, and Ramon "Speedy" Gonzalez hailed from the country of Honduras, and they were now the idols of the boys who listened to them over the radio every night. The kids not only longed to be like these men because they played baseball all the time, but they wanted to be like these men who left their poverty-stricken country to go on to a better life in America. Baseball was the only means for one of these boys to escape the poverty and working in the sugar cane fields all their life.

Fernando was the standout of the ballplayers in the city. He was fast, strong, and could catch a bullet from a gun with his glove. The young man's talents were recognized, and he was asked to join a team in the country's capital city to play ball. So at 16 years of age, Fernando knew that he had the chance of a lifetime. He decided to leave his mother, two brothers, little sister, and the sugar cane fields to play baseball. Wearing the only pair of clothes he had, Fernando set off to Yuscarán. On his eighteenth birthday, a professional scout from the Oakland A's signed this young man to play in their minor league system. Being used to playing with a broken glove on a rocky all-dirt infield, Fernando could catch anything when he was introduced to leather mitts and the smooth grass/dirt that was in the minor league stadiums of America. At bat, though, it took him a little while to get used to the faster pitching. However, after three years in the minors, he has able to improve his hitting dramatically. His efforts not only lead him to being named the Sun Valley Conference player of the year, but he was brought up to play in the majors the next season. Fernando had a great start as a rookie; his speed and excitement on the playing field made him fun to watch and made him a crowd favorite. The next season the Texas Rangers would offer him a 64 million dollar contract over 8 years. The exuberant Honduran quickly signed. A smile came upon his face when he realized that he now the man that he used to dream about as a boy. With his new paycheck, he decided to buy a plane ticket to Honduras to see his family for the first time since he left nearly 5 years ago.

Things back home were not what he expected. As soon as he stepped off the plane, the kids who listened to him on radio and the guys he grew up with welcomed him back to home. But not everybody warmly accepted Fernando back into town, for a quarter of the town's population had grown to hate Fernando. The were so jealous that he played baseball; they were jealous because he did not have to work in the fields in the hot sun; they were jealous that he left their country for America; they were jealous of the money he made; and they were jealous because he was the person that they dreamed of being.

Fernando's older brother Jorge had to tell him what happened. These jealous men took advantage of the Rodriquez family that was without a father in the household. Fernando's little sister was raped by some of these men. His younger brother by two years was stoned to death. The family house, the only thing the family owned, was burned down. And his mother aged dramatically within those five years because of all the stress she faced. The news broke Fernando's heart; while he was grieved at what happened, he also had an intense anger for what these men did to his family.

Raul, Fernando's close friend while growing up, came to Fernando one night and said that he knew who the men were who did those awful things to his family. He said that there were a lot of men that hated Fernando, and many of them joined in on the hateful events. But most of the events was done by five men. He said that they were the leaders who got everything started; they were the ones to strike the first and last blows. Raul said for a price he would get back at these men, even to go to the extent of killing these men for his friend. In the process of taking out the money to hand to Raul, Fernando decided that he could not to it. He could not repay evil for evil.

Fernando got together his family, and he was going to have them move back to America with him. But before he left, he gave a large sum of money to everyone in the city. A town where 5 cents can buy a meal for the family; he gave a dollar to everyone in the city, even to the ones that killed his brother and did such evil things to his family.

Fernando's story is not one we hear everyday, nor is it one that we expect. For as a society, we are bent on revenge. We have accepted the idea that we should get back at someone who has wronged us. Just look at the big screen, how many movies show evil acts and killings because men are getting revenge on how someone that has wronged them. And we the audience feel the same way: when the bad guy is shown doing evil, we in our minds already want revenge;

we want to give him what he deserves. But when did you see Jesus getting revenge on someone; He faced the bad guys of His time and they did some pretty evil things to him, but He never once tried to get back at them.

Don't get me wrong, it may be good for us to want to get back at a malicious leader that has killed thousands of innocent people. But what I am saying is, that it is not good to have this revenge-type attitude toward everything that we do not like in life.

People deserve revenge for all the evil that they have done, but we as Christians are not the ones to give it. We deserve hell for all the evil and sins that we have done/committed, but God does not want revenge on us – he wants to love us. Being in God's love, we should not want this form of hate in us; we should want to show kindness and mercy to others.

In your life, you should not want revenge or want to get back at someone; you should forgive. When someone wrongs you, do not show hate by wronging them back; forgive, and show them love. Showing love can be so much more powerful than any type of revenge. For when one wrongs you, they naturally expect for you to wrong them back. So when you show them love, they don't expect it – you throw them a curveball. When it sinks in that you forgave them, they feel bad for what they did to you – it hurts them that they hurt you. I guess, love does get back at that person – in a good way. Also, showing love leaves you not hating someone and that someone not hating you. In fact, now that person may feel like doing something nice back to you.

For example, there were two men, Julius and Tom that did not have a pleasant relationship with each other. The two did not really know each other except that they worked out at the fitness gym at the same time each day. At the gym, Tom would complain that Julius took to much time on certain machines and did not let others, like himself, use them; and Julius would complain that Tom always left heavy weights on the bars making others, like himself, move them.

Nick Shelton

One day Julius left his towel and cell phone on the spot where he normally left them, but Tom did not realize the cell phone was there on the towel, and he dropped one of his heavy dumbbells where the towel was lying. The 85-pound dumbbell smashed the cell phone. Julius ran over there and blessed Tom out; Julius was so mad he just picked up his towel and smashed cell phone and stomped out. The next day, Tom tried to avoid a confrontation with Julius at the gym, but he had already committed in a New Year's resolution that he would stay in shape by going to the gym everyday, and it was too hard with work to go to the gym at another time. So Tom went to the gym, and he saw Julius already in there. He tried to avoid him at first, but Julius eventually came to him and said, "Hey man, sorry about the way I acted yesterday; I probably went a little overboard. There was nothing hurt, it's just a cell phone; I could use a new one anyways." The startled Tom said, "Yeah-um- I'm sorry about that man." "Don't worry about it." And after that day, you could always see Tom making sure that he put up his heavy weights when he was done, and he was always real friendly to Julius.

How in the last week have you wanted revenge? How did you act to it?

How different would things be at the gym if Julius wanted revenge and did not apologize? How different would your life be if you did not want revenge and showed love?

Don't forget that kindness is the greatest way to get revenge.

How can we as people seek so much revenge, but then beg to God for mercy so that we may not get what we deserve?

Romans 12:19 Do not be overcome by evil, but overcome evil with good.

Leviticus 19:17 Do not hate your brother in your heart. Rebuke your neighbor frankly so you will not share in his guilt.

Proverbs 24:17 Do not gloat when your enemy falls; when he stumbles, do not let your heart rejoice

Matthew 5:46-48 If you love those who love you, what reward will you get? Are not even the tax collectors doing that? And if you greet only your brothers, what are you doing more than others? Do not even pagans do that? Be perfect, therefore, as your heavenly Father is perfect.

Luke 6:28 bless those who curse you, pray for those who mistreat you.

Romans 12:19,20 Do not take revenge, my friends, but leave room for God's wrath, for it is written: "It is mine to avenge; I will repay," says the Lord. On the contrary: "If your enemy is hungry, feed him; if he is thirsty, give him something to drink. In doing this, you will heap burning coals on his head."

Romans 15:2 Each of us should please his neighbor for his good, to build him up.

Little Bits of Heaven

Donald Caliparri was an American citizen whose parents were two Italian immigrants that came to America in hopes of living the American Dream. At a young age, Donald showed great creativity and a great artistic talent. His parents brought him up telling him that their family's ancestors must have stemmed from the great Italian artists like Da Vinci, Michelangelo, and Raphael. They told him that everyone from America to their home country of Italy would want to buy Donald's great works. They told him that he would be known as one of the greatest artist in the world. As a youth Donald painted many pieces, went to many artistic workshops, and dreamed of being that artist that his parents told him that he would be. At 18 years of age, Donald was accepted into one of the top artistic schools in the nation. At the school, Donald not only got to broaden his artistic capabilities, but also he met a fellow student that was a beautiful, young girl named Oceana. Donald would fall in love with this blonde girl from Destin, Florida; but more importantly, Donald would fall in love with this girl for more than her looks and similar artistic abilities. Donald fell in love with what Oceana loved and that was Jesus Christ. Though Donald's parents were members of a Roman Catholic Church back in Italy, when they moved to America, they slowly stopped going. Donald had never set foot in a church, let alone have any educational background about God. During a conversation of Renaissance painters portraying Jesus, their talks led to Oceana getting a chance to witness to Donald. That day changed Donald's life, and he has had Jesus in his heart ever since. Donald's paintings turned from images of gorgeous scenery and landscapes to portraits of Jesus and heaven. By his senior year, Donald had his life figured out. He was going to marry Oceana, and they would move to her hometown in Florida. They would sell their paintings and make millions. They would build a large house on the beach and live there. They travel would all across the country being honorary guests of arts shows and museums. For inspiration for their paintings, they would simply have to walk out in their backyard on the beach or take in the beautiful scenery from around this country that they had seen in their travels.

However, things did not quite work out as Donald pictured it. His paintings did not sell, or at least not at the price he expected. The two would struggle just to make a living; their paintings were selling at about the price it took them to create them. The two struggling artists did move down to Destin, but they could only afford a mobile home located 9 miles from the closest beach.

After 7 years and two children later, Donald and Oceana were still in that same situation in that same mobile home. Donald grew depressed; he was about to turn thirty years old, and he did not have the millions of dollars he dreamed, the fame that was supposed to come with it, or the perfect life that he pictured while he was in college. He did not understand why he could not have that life of greatness that he read in books that was to accompany being a Christian.

One afternoon, Donald walked alone barefooted on the beach watching the sunset. It was then when a flash of insight hit him. Donald realized that even though he did not have the money or fame that he had dreamed of, he did have perfect moments. For instance, he woke up to the most beautiful wife by his side as the sun trickled in their windows each morning; he kissed his two children every night before bed as they said, "I love you Daddy;" he was blessed with going to work everyday, as going to the beach to do what he loved – to paint; he had times of traveling to his parents home in New York City where they would eat to their heart's content some of the best Italian cooking in the world; he had the chance to put paintings of Jesus Christ in hundreds of homes; and he had this beautiful sunset. Donald realized that he had so many little bits of heaven in his life. It was then when he realized the he had the life of greatness that he always wanted.

Our lives too will have these little moments of heaven. Times like viewing a beautiful sunset, times of feeling loved by another, and times in which we experience that perfect peace with God. All of these things God gave to us to get a feel and glimpse of what heaven will be like. However, unlike these things, the joy of being in heaven will never end. When we run, we will not grow tired; those with bad eyes will have perfect vision; those without parents will have a father that will always love them; a tear will never fall; no pain will ever be felt; all our longings will be satisfied; and we will live in perfect peace in paradise. Although most do not realize it, we can experience a little bit of this greatness here on earth. When we go through our life, God will give to us moments when we get a warm feeling inside of us – we are having a second-long experience of what heaven is really like. All we must do to have this is - to keep a hope of heaven while on this earth. We must not keep our eyes focused on things of this world, but we must keep our focus on that of heaven. If you simply live a life of love under God's grace, these moments will find you, and with God in our lives, we can find these moments in everything.

Although I will not promise the success, wealth, fame, or having complete happiness all the time, I will promise you that you will have these moments of heaven, and from that you can experience complete joy. This joy, these moments should be enough to give us hope for a living a godly life while we long to experience the joy that is to come.

Another promise I can give you is that if you try to find this joy in money, fame, sex, drugs, or things of this world - you will always come short. All these things bring a short amount of pleasure, and then what? But God's love never ceases, and his love completely satisfies our heart. In God, you can find pleasure in anything, and everyday with God should be a blessing to your soul. If we focus on earth we will get earth and all its troubles; if we focus on heaven, we will get little bits of heaven and all its joys.

What can we do in life? We can enjoy God in everything, and in everything we can experience the joy of heaven.

Have you enjoyed these little moments of heaven in your life? Would you trade these things for anything? Let these things be a reminder to you of heaven, and how you want nothing more than to be in heaven.

On all our days here on earth, we can enjoy loving God and having little moments of heaven.

We may never reach the greatness of what we once dreamed, but we have the hope of heaven which is far greater than what we could ever dream.

Colossians 3:1-4 Since, then, you have been raised with Christ, set your hearts on things above, where Christ is seated at the right hand of God. et your minds on things above, not on earthly things. For you died, and your life is now hidden with Christ in God. When Christ, who is your life, appears, then you also will appear with him in glory.

Psalm 73:25 Whom have I in heaven but you? And earth has nothing I desire besides you

I Corinthians 15:49 And just as we have borne the likeness of the earthly man, so shall we bear the likeness of the man from heaven.

2 Corinthians 4:18 So we fix our eyes not on what is seen, but on what is unseen. For what is seen is temporary, but what is unseen is eternal.

2 Corinthians 5:2,5 Meanwhile we groan, longing to be clothed with our heavenly dwelling,

Now it is God who has made us for this very purpose and has given us the Spirit as a deposit, guaranteeing what is to come

Colossians 1:5,6 the faith and love that spring from the hope that is stored up for you in heaven and that you have already heard about in the word of truth, the gospel **6**that has come to you. All over the world this gospel is bearing fruit and growing, just as it has been doing among you since the day you heard it and understood God's grace in all its truth.

I Peter 1:3,4 In his great mercy he has given us new birth into a living hope through the resurrection of Jesus Christ from the dead, **4**and into an inheritance that can never perish, spoil or fade—kept in heaven for you

I John 3:3 Everyone who has this hope in him purifies himself, just as he is pure.

Immovable Objects

Charles Atlas was an English scientist who lived at the end of the 19th century. His 5 foot 6 inch frame and thin-framed spectacles gave him an appearance of a typical scientist. However, this 140-pound scientist was actually a world champion bodybuilder. His secret? It was not the illegal steroids that Olympic athletes and baseball players have gotten in trouble for using today; it was a system of building strength through isometric exercises.

The basic principle behind isometric exercises is to push, pull, or lift something that you cannot. For example, Charles' routine consisted of pushing against a wall of his house as hard as he could, for as many times as he could. He then would change positions so that he worked every muscle in his body. For example, Charles would position himself in the middle of doorways, grab the handles of a 500-pound metal tank, or find other immovable objects like boulders, trees, etc. He would position himself and push/pull in dozens of different ways, allowing him to work every muscle in his body. People around town thought this man was insane when he went grunting, sweating, and straining to push a wall. I can imagine the looks on their faces when people offered to help the struggling Charles to move the 500 lb. tank, and he replied to their offer, "No thank you, I am exercising."

Though Charles may have looked ridiculous, his body showed the results from his isometric workout. By constantly working his muscles, Charles' muscles grew bigger and stronger in attempt to do what it took to move the wall. While Charles would never move a wall, his isometric system of working out, greatly improved his strength and revolutionized the idea of strength training.

In several national competitions, Charles would prove himself stronger than men twice his size (they did not have weights back then, so they did things like: measure how far one could throw, hold, or carry a heavy object). Charles also won the national bodybuilding competition for his weight class.

I am sure Charles once looked into the mirror and saw a squawky, nerdy figure who could only amount to being a white-collar lab scientist, but through hard work and determination, he proved to be a success in something nobody could imagine.

How many instances in your life do you feel like you are trying your best at something but you are making no or little progress. You don't understand it; you are trying/working at something with all your heart, but it feels like you are getting nowhere – like you were pushing against a wall. However, as one can see with Charles' example, just because we feel like we are doing nothing or getting nowhere, this does not mean that something is not changing. What we do not realize is that we are building character and are changing something - it just may not be that immovable object in front of us. This principle correlates to so many things in life, but let us look at it from a spiritual perspective.

Say you have a friend that you know does not believe in God, and you are trying to show him the Truth. You can spend hours talking to him debating and giving evidence on why he should/needs to believe, but he remains stubborn and will not listen. You may feel like any efforts are in vain, and you are just wasting your time trying to move this immovable object. But in the process you are building up your spiritual "muscles." In order to explain to him what Christianity is all about, you must know what you are talking about yourself, so you adapt by learning more scripture and becoming more familiar with God. Not only are you helping out yourself but others also. Other Christians see you doing this for your friend, and this may spur them to likewise reach out and share the gospel to unbelievers. Other unbelievers like your friend, may see how much you care for your friend and how you show love to him, and this may lead them to sparking an interest that leads to God. Plus, if you were ever in a situation like that again with another person, you would know how to better explain what you believe and why they should believe.

Our problem, nowadays, is that we want results too fast. Charles worked for two years at his isometric exercises before he went to any bodybuilding or strength competition. But we go on a diet for a week and want results. We talk to an unbeliever once and get discouraged if he doesn't come to Christ. We give up on our dreams because we get discouraged from failing a few times, or we receive criticisms from others.

There is nothing too great that we cannot do. The harder we try the more our bodies adapt to trying to reach it. This is why Charles' body got stronger; this why the intelligent who read books all day, grow smarter; this is why the rich who focus on money, become richer; and the righteous who focus on God, become closer to God. This is why I repeatedly tell people to follow your dreams and love God with all your heart. For even if you are giving your all and going nowhere with it, you are adapting to become what you are striving for.

Have you had any instances, now that you look back, that you pushed, pulled, and gave your all? How has it impacted your life?

In what areas of your life have you done this? Is it in the areas that matter most to you?

If you feel like you have not done these isometric exercises in your life or have not done this enough, find what God wants for you to do in your life, and start today to attempt to move the immovable.

You may not have success, but after much time of work, your "muscles" will be sure to show. You may never move that wall in your life, but you can always get stronger trying.

Colossians 1:11 being strengthened with all power according to his glorious might so that you may have great endurance and patience, and joyfully giving thanks to the Father, who has qualified you to share in the inheritance of the saints in the kingdom of light

James 1:4 Perseverance must finish its work so that you may be mature and complete, not lacking anything

1 Samuel 12:23,24 As for me, far be it from me that I should sin against the LORD by failing to pray for you. And I will teach you the way that is good and right. But be sure to fear the LORD and serve him faithfully with all your heart; consider what great things he has done for you.

Romans 5:3-5 Not only so, but we also rejoice in our sufferings, because we know that suffering produces perseverance; perseverance, character; and character, hope. And hope does not disappoint us, because God has poured out his love into our hearts by the Holy Spirit, whom he has given us.

We were not created for Earth

In the 1993 film, *Free Willy,* a large Orca whale named Willy
is captured from the wild to be a star attraction of a marine life
amusement park. The whale is put in a tank where it is taught to do
tricks and playful antics to entertain the people. Willy is surrounded
by playful kids laughing and having fun, but it does not take long
for Willy to become discontent. Willy is doing things normal whales
did not have to do, and it is in a closed habitat that whales are not
accustomed to. Since it is in a closed environment, Willy's large
dorsal fin begins to flop down from not using it. Before long, the
whale grows a stubborn/antisocial behavior in which it does not
perform its tricks for the people, and it is disobedient to the trainers.
The owners of the amusement parks and the crowds that show up
to watch, both grow upset with this large un-cooperating creature.
But a young boy (named Jesse in the movie) embraces the whale
and feels his pain. Jesse hears of plots of hurting the whale from
eavesdropping on some of the park's officials; a plot that plans to
injure or kill the whale in order to collect a large sum of insurance
money. Jesse then proceeds to shift all his attention to saving Willy.
With the help of a friendly Native American friend, Jesse takes the
hurting whale back to the sea. Then in one of the most memorable
moments in movie's history, Willy takes a dramatic leap from over
the rocks, on which Jesse is standing, hurling itself from the harbor

to the sea. Then at that moment, Jesse, the whale, and even the audience is pleased about Willy's return home.

We as humans are just like Willy – we will never be truly happy here on earth. We were not created to be of this world.

All the things we do are like Willy's tricks – we simply were not created for that. And sin does exactly like the closed environment did with Willy when his fin drooped - it completely changes us because we are in an environment that we were not created for. Earth is just our temporary home, until we get to make that "leap" into our real home in heaven.

To remind me of this, I keep a laminated card in my wallet that says, "Citizen of Heaven" and on the back: "Green Card for Earth"

Most of us have not yet fully grasped the concept of living for eternity. We mostly have a short term and self-centered outlook on life. However, as many theologians have pointed out: all our days on earth are just the cover or title page of a book that only describes the unlimited number of pages inside.

We always hear of how there is so much wrong in the world and how life is not fair, but life is this way because of our own wrongdoings and what comes from sin. We base so much around money, being loved by someone, and having fun. When we fall short of our expectations (and we as humans always do), we become depressed and say how we hate life. But as Christians, we must continually be looking toward the goal (which is heaven). We should be trying to live our lives just like it is - an audition for the main play.

How foolish must our emotions and actions look like to God, when we get upset over the trivial things of this earth, for these things will mean nothing when we are in heaven. We as Christians cannot be focused on all the things of this world.

Just think about it – what does it matter?

Years from now, it will not matter how many friends you have, where you live, how much money you make a year, or what kind of car you drive. For one day, you will have to leave this world and everything in it all behind. All that we will have is a soul that can be either completely full of sin, or completely spotless from our sins being washed away.

Life is like a long journey, in which it is our pursuit to make it to a seemingly impossible goal. You can try to reach the goal by trying to obtain the best gear/equipment (money, possessions, other worldly things) and try to make the most out of your journey. Or you can chose the path of God, following where he leads you, knowing that you will one day reach where you were created to be.

Philippians 3:20 But our citizenship is in heaven. And we eagerly await a Savior from there, the Lord Jesus Christ, who, by the power that enables him to bring everything under his control, will transform our lowly bodies so that they will be like his glorious body.

Psalm 39:4 Show me, O LORD, my life's end and the number of my days; let me know how fleeting is my life.

Psalm 90:5,6 You sweep men away in the sleep of death; they are like the new grass of the morning—

though in the morning it springs up new, by evening it is dry and withered.

Psalm 119:19 I am a stranger on earth; do not hide your commands from me.

I Corinthians 7:31b For this world in its present form is passing away.

I Corinthians 9:25 Everyone who competes in the games goes into strict training. They do it to get a crown that will not last; but we do it to get a crown that will last forever.

I Peter 1:17 Since you call on a Father who judges each man's work impartially, live your lives as strangers here in reverent fear.

Dedicated to the Lord

Buddy Cameron was a long distance runner from Townsend, Connecticut. Buddy was described by everybody of the town as the definition of the word *dedicated*. Whether it has snowing, raining, lightning, or 100° outside, Buddy would be running every morning at 6:00 a.m. Buddy ran in marathon, 5/10K, and triathlon races all over the northeast. Running was what Buddy truly loved. Every morning, no matter whether Buddy was stressed, mad, or unhappy about something else in his life, everyone in the small town could still see the joy on the face of this 32-year-old man when he was simply doing what he loved doing. While others balked at the idea of running 26.2 miles, Buddy loved it. Some people would look at this man and question why would anyone do this each and every day. But Buddy quickly pointed out that it: relived all his stress, let him plan out his day, made him feel better, gave him the satisfaction that he was doing something good for his body, gave him a chance to see the beautiful town during the quiet time of the morning, and it was simply what he liked to do. To the residents of Townsend, CT, Buddy was part of the town. Going to work everybody would honk their horns and give shouts of praise while Buddy was doing what he loved.

So is the evidence of your love to God this apparent?

We live in a culture where there are many fads and many things that hold our attention for a short while. Like how we try that low-carb diet, how we try to help others, how we spend our time with a distant friend, and how we buy that new piece of exercise equipment. At first, we take on these tasks with such exuberance, thinking we are turning over a new leaf that will change our life for the better, but look where we end up. We stop the diet and using the treadmill, and our bodies turn back to what they were; we stop talking to that one friend and our relationship goes back to what is was; and we stop trying to help others and we turn back to thinking on selfish principles.

So how much is this like your spiritual life? I think we all can admit this - we hear a powerful sermon and we want to change our lives so much in a certain way, but by the end of the week this excitement has dwindled, and by a month's time, we are as if we were in the first place before the sermon.

But for God's word and spirit to root in us we, must be dedicated – just like Buddy. Following God is what we should "just love doing." When we dedicate ourselves to God and really love him, everyone (just like they saw in Buddy) should see this love in us.

What makes a man's character is what he loves. And the time he puts into this love, will dictate how much of this character is noticeable. For example when we see a man with huge body-builder like muscles, we see that has shown much love into lifting weights and eating proper nutrition, and we can infer that he puts a large amount of time doing it. The same can be true of an architect by examining what kind, how many, and quality of the structures that he has built. The same is also true in our spiritual life. When we truly love God and spend much of our time with him, our "muscles" and "buildings" will be seen – we will be seen as dedicated by everyone else and by God.

But so many of us are unwilling to be dedicated. One claims that being dedicated to the Lord: "will make me standout in the workplace," "will not get me any friends," "will make me stop committing a certain sin(s) that I enjoy doing," or "be a hindrance to my job/personal goals." But having God in your life will not hinder anything; truly having God in your life will only multiply your blessings. And any group or person that is not willing to accept your closeness to God is not worth your time at all.

Being dedicated is not about wearing ugly Christian t-shirts, preventing you from hanging around certain friends (unless those friends constantly tempting you or causes you to sin), and being at Church front row every Sunday. Being dedicated is when you love God so much, that everyone can tell that you are a follower of Jesus. Being dedicated is doing what you know is right no matter how much you have to give up. Being dedicated is following what you are called to do no matter how much it hurts.

When you are dedicated, you do not see what you are giving up or feel the pain because the love of the object that you desire is greater than such things. You are so focused on that which you love that everything else is just a blur.

So how dedicated are you as a Christian?

Does the amount of time you donate to God, show you are dedicated?

Does your willingness to give up something for the sake of God, show that you are dedicated?

Does your actions and what everyone else sees in you, show that you are dedicated?

Does the love that you pour out to God each day, show that you are dedicated?

Does doing what you truly love, show you are dedicated?

It says in the Word that a Christian's body should be a temple for the Lord. So, is your temple been used for other things – or is it being dedicated to the Lord?

Don't let your Christian life be this ongoing fad, spend your time by loving God and everyone will see the definition of dedication.

I Corinthians 7:35 I am saying this for your own good, not to restrict you, but that you may live in a right way in undivided devotion to the Lord.

I Corinthians 6:19, 20 Do you not know that your body is a temple of the Holy Spirit, who is in you, whom you have received from God? You are not your own; you were bought at a price. Therefore honor God with your body

Leviticus 11:44 I am the LORD your God; consecrate yourselves and be holy, because I am holy

I Corinthians 9:24 Do you not know that in a race all the runners run, but only one gets the prize? Run in such a way as to get the prize

2 Corinthians 8:3-5 For I testify that they gave as much as they were able, and even beyond their ability. Entirely on their own, they urgently pleaded with us for the privilege of sharing in this service to the saints. And they did not do as we expected, but they gave themselves first to the Lord and then to us in keeping with God's will

2 Timothy 4:7 I have fought the good fight, I have finished the race, I have kept the faith.

Having Love

Rounasi was a man from the Cragel tribe that inhabited the southern lands in Malex. Malex was a land in earth, not earth now, but earth in future years. In the lands of Malex, life is a struggle to gain land. Good land or "gomb," as they call it, is scarce, for barren wastelands scatter the earth. The world centers on war; life is a continuance of swapping of land by tribes. There is no countries; there is no peace; and there is no love.

Rounasi was born a warrior. This means his purpose for life was to gain lands for his country. Warriors were the most respected members of the society, and the warriors determined their tribe's fate. They were the ones called to fight the ever-constant war. War for them is not as we think of it in our time, it is more like a sports competition that involved objects, weapons, strategies, or teams. The winner of the war won the other tribe's land and spoils; the loser would have to give up a choice of 10 human sacrifices that would be burned to the other tribe's gods.

Rounasi was a gifted fighter that was unparalleled by anyone of his tribe. At age 13, he was introduced to the battlefield. By 18, he had become the tribe's strongest warrior; he would become the only one that could save his tribe from their powerful enemies. Every time Rounasi would go to war, he would have this feeling, a feeling deep down in him that he could not explain. He told the priests of this feeling and they called this the gods stirring up inside of him. They regarded him as chosen by the gods.

One day as Rounasi was resting in a field, something came to him. It was not a dream, it was not a vision, it was not something he came up with in his imagination; it was something that just came to him – it was love. He understood it. He finally knew what that was inside of him when he won a victory against his enemies. The idea consumed him.

He told others, but they did not comprehend. He would continue to experience the feeling on the battlefield, but he knew that there was something more than this feeling. There had to be a source.

Rounasi would recruit some of his friends, and they would leave their tribe and search for Rounasi's mystery: the source of love. Everywhere they went, there was no sign of it; all the world was just the same – one tribe fighting another, one tribe gaining land only to lose it back the next day to another tribe. The group grew weary from their travels, and they felt like they could not travel any further. This is when a light beamed down from the sky and shone brightly in front of Rounasi and his men. All others were afraid of this scene, but Rounasi knew that this was the source, and he stepped into the light. In the brief moment that he was in there, he saw the world and how everything that it was doing was wrong. He saw the fighting, he saw the worshipping to the gods, and he saw that this was not what life was about. Then it came to him, he saw It. The light blinded his eyes, but he was attracted like a magnet to Its splendor. He had found It; It was now in him; and It would now lead him, as he went out to try and change the world.

Could you imagine life without love? What if life was centered on things that it was not supposed to do? What if we chased meaningless things and did things that we were not indented to do? Or is that how life is now? Is it not how you have once lived your life?

Without coming to "the source" (that being God) our lives are nothing. We wander around this place that we do not know, and do what we do not understand.

We travel on a journey, but do not know where we are heading. Instead of trying to reach our journey's destination, we just try to make the most of our journey. However, there is a map, there is a Guide, and there is a Way to get to our destination. It is found in God.

So on your journey, have you stepped into the Light?

Has The Light exposed you to all the wrong in your life and in this world?

Are you drawer nearer to the Light?

Is the Light changing you, as you are changing the world?

We should find ourselves in this Light – The source of Love. As we draw nearer to the Source, its love grows in us. This love - the feeling inside of you that grips you, making you want to do something to cause the same feeling in another - should always be present in your life. For we no longer live in the dark but in the Light. We are no longer roaming around in the dark not knowing where to go; we are now in the Light where our eyes can see, enabling us to run unhindered towards the goal. Your life now has meaning, it has joy, and it has love.

Think of what you have learned and how you have grown in these previous weeks.

How has love come into your life? Would you ever want to turn back to a life without it? Has it not made your life more complete? Has it not brought you more joy? Has this love forever changed your life?

I would like to bid you farewell, asking that if you don't remember any other thing from these devotionals, remember this one thing - love.

Psalm 23:6 Surely goodness and love will follow me all the days of my life, and I will dwell in the house of the LORD forever.

John 8:12 When Jesus spoke again to the people, he said, "I am the light of the world. Whoever follows me will never walk in darkness, but will have the light of life."

1 Corinthians 13:13 And now these three remain: faith, hope and love. But the greatest of these is love.

2 Corinthians 4:4 The god of this age has blinded the minds of unbelievers, so that they cannot see the light of the gospel of the glory of Christ, who is the image of God.

Psalm 18:1,2 I love you, O LORD, my strength. The LORD is my rock, my fortress and my deliverer; my God is my rock, in whom I take refuge.

Matthew 22:37-39 Jesus replied: "'Love the Lord your God with all your heart and with all your soul and with all your mind.' This is the first and greatest commandment. And the second is like it: 'Love your neighbor as yourself

John 3:19-21 This is the verdict: Light has come into the world, but men loved darkness instead of light because their deeds were evil. Everyone who does evil hates the light, and will not come into the light for fear that his deeds will be exposed. But whoever lives by the truth comes into the light, so that it may be seen plainly that what he has done has been done through God."

Ephesians 3:17-19 And I pray that you, being rooted and established in love, may have power, together with all the saints, to grasp how wide and long and high and deep is the love of Christ, and to know this love that surpasses knowledge—that you may be filled to the measure of all the fullness of God

Ephesians 5:8-10 For you were once darkness, but now you are light in the Lord. Live as children of light (for the fruit of the light consists in all goodness, righteousness and truth) and find out what pleases the Lord.

Jude 21 Keep yourselves in God's love as you wait for the mercy of our Lord Jesus Christ to bring you to eternal life.

Source Page

1. Scriptures:

Scriptures quotations taken from the HOLY BIBLE, NEW INTERNATIONAL VERSION®. Copyright © 1973,1978,1884 by International Bible Society. Used by permission of Zondervan Publishing House. All rights reserved.

2. Sujo devotional:

John, Sujo. <u>Do you know where you are going?</u>. New York: Lantern Books, 2002.

3. Greek Pride devotional:

Lewis, C.S. Mere Christianity. New York: Harper Collins Publishing, 1996.

4. Assembling the Body of Christ devotional:

Casting Crowns. "If We Are the Body." Reunion Records, 2003

Printed in the United States
23936LVS00001B/308